# 5-Minute
## Diet Book

# 5-Minute
## Diet Book

## Ajay Rochester

NEW
HOLLAND

First published in 2010 by New Holland Publishers (Australia) Pty Ltd
Sydney • Auckland • London • Cape Town

www.newholland.com.au

1/66 Gibbes Street Chatswood NSW 2067 Australia
218 Lake Road Northcote Auckland New Zealand
86 Edgware Road London W2 2EA United Kingdom
80 McKenzie Street Cape Town 8001 South Africa

National Library of Australia Cataloguing-in-Publication Data:

Rochester, A. J.

The 5 minute diet book / Ajay Rochester

ISBN 9781741109986 (pbk.)

1. Health.
2. Food habits—Psychological aspects.
3. Weight loss.
4. Nutrition—Psychological aspects.

613.25

Publisher: Diane Jardine
Publishing manager: Lliane Clarke
Cover Photograph: Gaye Gerard/Getty Images. Hair and make up by Georgie Eisdel. Shirt by Charlie Brown.
Project editor: Talina McKenzie
Proofreader: Meryl Potter
Designer: Amanda Tarlau
Cover design: Amanda Tarlau
Production manager: Olga Dementiev
Printer:  Ligare Book Printers, Australia

*For Mardi, Sarah, Lauren, Yvette, Suz, Stav, all my girls in Healthy Body Club and for Oprah—because we all need a little help some times in our lives.*

*Kaizziepops: I love you!*

# CONTENTS

# THE END OF YOUR OLD SELF

**Are you sick and tired of feeling sick and tired? Do you wake up in the morning, roll over and groan into the pillow knowing this is just another day trapped in a never-ending cycle of self-abuse? How many days, weeks or years are you going to promise yourself that it is the last piece of pizza, the last takeout, the last day of not exercising, the last day of too many wines followed by a midnight feast followed by too many wines followed by a greasy breakfast? The merry-go-round is spinning out of control and you have absolutely no idea how to stop it before killing yourself .**

And then that stupid voice tells you that since you started the day badly you might as well end it badly—although maybe it's better to wait until next week, or the first day of the next month, or perhaps the first day of next year, or when Venus is crossed with Uranus… I'll tell you what should be in Uranus: my foot swiftly delivered to your butt so you can wake up and smell the roses. This is the END of your old life right now, this very second.

You should be waking up excited by the promise a new day brings, embracing your good health and ready to pursue all the wonderful adventures life has in store for you. Life is meant to be lived and you are meant to be loved—not only by others but by yourself. Change will only come when you start treating yourself with the respect you deserve (NOW). You have to take that very first step (NOW). The sooner you start the better your life will be, so why wait for tomorrow, next week or, God forbid, next year?

Guess what? You've already started just by reading this far. You might as well follow through because what other option is there? Put your hands in the air and back away from the fridge. Go on, you can do it. You are stronger than you think. Sure, that chocolate cake may help you forget that your boyfriend just left you for a younger, thinner, blonder woman but the only thing you'll get in the custody battle are thighs the size of life boats. Trust me, it's not worth that little moment of what you think is 'instant gratification' otherwise known as another bullshit expression called 'comfort eating'.

I actually don't subscribe to the 'happiness lies in the smallest pair of pants on the rack' ideology. I have weighed as little as 40 kilos and as much as 150 kilos, and until I dealt with healing my head, my heart, and a lifetime of bad habits, no amount of weight loss was ever going to complete me. Why do you think most people who lose a lot of weight put it all back on again? They realise they are still unhappy, seek happiness in food, shrink again, wind up still starving (of self love and hunger)…round and round and round it goes, where it stops nobody knows!

And while we are being honest, let's get the question of my own weight out of the way. There has been a lot of speculation about how much I weighed at my heaviest and the truth is: I have no idea. My scales only ever measured up to 110 kilos. I remember getting fatter and fatter, not understanding why the number never went up and deluding myself that no matter what I ate I no longer put on weight.

Maybe scales should just measure in words after you pass the 100 kilo mark: fat cow, you've gotta be joking, please hop off me now, aren't you dead yet? Maybe that would make us want to save ourselves sooner. God knows I didn't want to know the truth, and my faulty scales aided and abetted me in my attempted suicide—otherwise known as death by chocolate. It's a frightening reflection of the growing obesity epidemic when domestic scales are now capable of weighing people over 250 kilos, a number previously only able to be calculated on industrial scales.

'It's a frightening reflection of the growing obesity epidemic when domestic scales are now capable of weighing people over 250 kilos.'

After four years as host of The Biggest Loser Australia and eight years of helping women save their lives with the online support group www.myhealthybodyclub.com, I have become pretty good at estimating how much someone weighs before they step on the scales. Being height challenged (I blame being underloved as a baby—I only grew to 5 foot 1 inch) and having bloated to a point where even my pictures fell off the wall, I can only estimate that I was around 150 kilos at the pinnacle of self-neglect. My eating was so out of control my cereal bowl came with a lifeguard. I was so big even my clothes had stretch marks. When eating out, if the waiter offered me the menu I would say, 'Yes please!' And while I can make jokes about it now, it was no laughing matter.

I was a heart attack waiting to happen. Even more tragic, I wasn't just ridiculously fat, I was the walking, talking, physical embodiment of my own self-hatred, soul-aching sadness, desperate loneliness and utter despair. I lived in a constant state of self-abuse and denial, perpetuated by the paralysing fear of how it might end. I didn't have the first clue how to save myself from the miserable existence I had settled for. Most of all, I didn't believe I deserved any better.

Don't get me wrong: I'm not blaming being fat for my misery. Fat was just the side effect of how I felt about myself. It made no difference which jeans I was squeezing myself into: circus-sized or flea-sized. It all led to the same sad place: waking up each day loathing the body I lived in, wishing for anybody else's life and, on the worst days, wishing it (meaning me) would all just go away. Some days I wanted to die. See the irony? I wanted to take my life because I had the kind of body that was killing me.

I went from trying to bury my feelings in food, and myself in fat, to putting all my hope in the hands of quick fixes. I became the diet industry's perfect worshipper: brainwashed to believe that my only path to true happiness lay in following their ways, no matter how crazy they sounded.

I became powerless, foolishly buying every pre-packaged, delivered to your door, holy grail of weight loss available for only five hundred payments of $59.95 plus postage. I would still be making payments years after they became unopened, unused relics. My garage became the graveyard of good diets gone bad.

My entire life revolved around either being on a diet—which involved massive amounts of suffering—or being off my diet—which involved massive amounts of guilt because I was not putting myself through the massive amounts of suffering.

In my extensive career as a diet addict you could say I earned my PhD in extreme regimes. I have starved, binged, dieted, detoxed, ab-blasted, stair-mastered, boot-camped, hip-hopped, pill-popped and yoyoed my way from a size 8 to a size 30 and back again. I have eaten whole food groups, partial food groups, no food groups, fruits, soups, salads, syrups, shakes, bars, pre-packaged, natural, organic, fresh, frozen, reheated, protein-treated, powdered, puffed, pulverised, freeze-dried, deep fried and magnified. There have been times when I survived eating less than an ant, then binged on enough to feed an entire football team and their fans.

I totally outgrew 'One Size Fits All' (no it doesn't!); I bypassed 'Free Size' altogether and binged my way into 'Free Willy Save the Whales Better Buy a Circus Tent Cause That is All That

Fits You' size—sometimes referred to as PLUS size. Which actually stands for Please give me Liposuction, my Underpants are Sumo-sized.

It was not until I actually stopped 'dieting' (i.e. gave up strict, unhealthy regimes) that I finally lost weight—and for the first time ever, it didn't bounce back a few weeks later. And I'm not talking about a little off my chin; I lost the weight of two whole people from my body and, beating the odds of dieters around the world, I can categorically say I have beaten obesity forever. I will never again stay awake at night, wondering if that heart pain is indigestion or the heart attack I knew was coming.

That was almost ten years ago and I have not looked back once. Deciding to stop 'dieting', and committing to living healthily instead was the best thing I have ever done.

These days I have absolutely no idea how much I weigh. I don't care. I chose long-term health, fitness and fulfilment over a race to be a number on a scale by a certain date. I wear anything from an Australian size 8 to 12 depending on the label or brand. Every day I wake up joyful that I am not weighed down by obesity or by self-hatred of my body. I am free, healthy and happy. I have good and bad days just like anyone, but I also have more days to enjoy because I am no longer killing myself with too much or too little food. Yay!

I no longer lie awake worrying if my life will end with a crane lifting me out of my house *What's Eating Gilbert Grape* style. I no longer agonise over having something yummy, I do not silently high-five myself for going hungry for sustained periods and I do not punish myself (either emotionally or by extreme exercise) when I eat. I can honestly say I have found the lifelong tools to beat obesity, anorexia, self-abuse and the low self-esteem that follows all of them. I found the balance that works for me and I want to share it with everyone who wants to live a healthier, happier, more peaceful, nurturing, loving life.

But here's the thing: this is a permanent commitment to living a different way, a healthier, happier way—not some instant pre-packaged line of BS that promises (and fails) to instantly cure you of a lifetime of weight issues.

I'm not saying my life is perfect, but when good days go bad I no longer turn to three boxes of chocolates to counsel me. Instead, I reach for the trusty little book of techniques I have collected over the last ten years. I set myself easy-to-achieve tasks to learn healthier habits and stop the negative thought patterns that kept me trapped in obesity for years. Instead of doing just one thing (e.g. replacing three meals a day with a shake to magically solve all my problems), I give myself 100 easy ways of doing things differently. I feel better, which in turn makes me treat myself better, and before I know it I'm out of the negative spin cycle.

You know that feeling when everything just seems so bad you don't know how to get started, let alone even contemplate crossing the finish line? This is exactly the point I want to make! Do not think about the end. Don't even fret about how to begin. Don't think about the what ifs, the how tos, the how long or even how hard it may be. Don't think about whether you can do it or where you will find the magical motivation to achieve your goals. Forget about the bigger picture because it doesn't exist. A journey of a thousand steps is just that: one step a thousand times.

All you have to do right now is just one thing. You already know how to lose weight. Seriously, you know you do. Calories in, calories out, exercise. Sure, if it were that easy we'd all look like Miranda Kerr and the world would indeed be a beautiful and perfect place. It's not that easy. You have to toil on bad habits, negative mindsets and unhelpful beliefs to make a permanent positive change. Work from the inside to change your backside.

Devote just five minutes, right now, to change. Then devote another five minutes and another and another. See each five minutes as a building block for your future, creating a solid foundation for the better, stronger, longer life you are about to lead.

Devote just five minutes at a time to learning something new, thinking differently, or doing something better than yesterday. Invest your energy once a day, once a week or once a month: whatever you are ready for. Focus on doing something today rather than worrying about everything you have to do tomorrow. When you take away the pressure of setting a goal that is impossible to imagine, you can focus on the achievable goal of being 'healthier' (instead of 'skinny' or 'a size 6') NOW.

'All you have to do right now is just one thing. You already know how to lose weight.'

Guess what? If you decide to be just a little bit healthier today, you are already successful. If tomorrow you decide to do that and monitor your emotions, learning how poor choices can affect your mood and energy, then you have been successful two days in a row. If you decide that over the next week you will focus on being happy and fulfilled, instead of determining how you feel by whether or not your body is 'good enough' then guess what? You have been successful.

Imagine if an athlete decided at the start of their career that was as good as they would ever be, therefore there was no point training to be the best? The true definition of failure is not trying.

Imagine the joy of being successful every single day, even when you make mistakes (otherwise known as lessons), rather than gambling your whole investment on a single moment when you step on a scale, try on a dress or stand next to someone thinner than you. How exhausting! You are doing this the wrong way about. Work on the inside and the outside will respond. Be happy now. Love yourself now. Do NOT put your life and self-respect on hold until you think you deserve it because you fit into a miniskirt. People will not stand at your casket and comment on what a great body you had. The measure of your life will be the love you have, from others and for yourself.

I will never be obese again, because I found a way to fill my life with something other than food. I offer you the tools to treat yourself with the love and respect each of us deserves—no matter what size we are. Fill your heart, watch your body shrink, save yourself thousands of dollars and countless hours of suffering.

Don't even get me started on whose idea it was that sporting a healthy body means having to go without the things you love, agonising over every bite that goes in and spending every spare hour away from your friends and family working off calories. No pain no gain? Who said that—Attila the Hun? What if I said that you can enjoy your life and have a healthy body as well? You can have your cake and eat it too, and you don't have to survive on rabbit food just so you can wear a Playboy bunny outfit.

I'm not saying you can continue to have KFC on your speed dial and sport hot and spicy legs of your own, but there is no point being a beautiful corpse if life's been a misery. It's all about choices and balance, and at all times loving, honouring and respecting yourself.

I dropped eight dress sizes in just one year by tackling every issue, bad habit or ill-informed belief I'd hidden behind my whole life, taking it just five minutes at a time. That was the sum total of my investment. It was cheaper and easier than any 'diet' I had ever tried. You can do the same—and don't even tell me you can't afford it. Everyone can take five minutes a day to live a better life.

Let me say this: you have inside of you everything you need to make a change for the better.

You can crash diet your way into a tiny dress for summer but unless you learn the tools to stay fit and healthy, you will be going up and down in weight and on and off a diet for the rest of your life. The quick-fix industry locks you into the diet merry-go-round. Lose it quickly, put it back on (plus some). Try again, take it off in two weeks and put even more back on in three. Before you know it you have lost and gained three times your weight, you hate your life, you can see no way of fixing it quickly or easily so you figure there's no way to do it at all. You convince yourself you are a failure and unworthy of a decent life, so you give up altogether and bury your depression in anything you can get Supersized. Studies have shown that 90 per cent of people who lose significant amounts of weight rapidly put it all back on, plus ten per cent, within a year. It's not your fault! You are just another well-rounded figure in a diet game that was designed to convince you that you can't and won't ever do it on your own.

Guess what? Congratulate yourself on finally being in the perfect place to change your life for the better. You have graduated from fat camp to the school of life, and you are finally ready to put your past and your fat arse behind you. You are going to rebuild a healthier, happier you that feels and looks good. Even though in the back of your mind you are wondering how long this will take, all you need to know is the change is already happening, you are already a success. Now just keep reading.

If you're freaking out about how much weight you have to lose, think of your transformation this way. How do you eat an elephant? One bite at a time. It's that simple. This book is filled with tiny bites of wellness that will change the way you think about yourself, the way you behave on a day-to-day basis and heal the relationship you have with your heart, mind, body and spirit.

Before we move forward, you have to throw out every pre-conceived idea you have of dieting. Have you noticed that even lap band surgery patients put weight back on if they don't change the way they live? It's like restoring a Ferrari and only having enough money for the body parts. It might look fast, sexy and fire engine red, but unless there's a working engine underneath the bonnet you are going nowhere fast.

There is nothing quick about a quick fix. I understand the appeal of drinking and eating whatever you want for months then sipping some magic syrup for ten days straight, somehow managing to stand up without falling over in the dream dress at your sister's wedding. But have two wines on an empty stomach and you'll wind up with the fire department having to crowbar your tongue off the ice sculpture of Cupid, with no memory of 'that speech' that has your entire family and the in-laws not speaking to you. You are then so depleted of food you go on an insatiable binge for three weeks straight, sleepwalk your way through five fast food drive-throughs and wake up one morning surrounded by the wrappers of fifteen burgers you have no memory of eating. Or was that just me?

I have been there done that and been there done fat—and I have the stretch marks to prove it. I recently had more than five kilos of excess skin cut off my body. I was walking around in the skin of a much bigger person and it took me almost ten years to finally accept she was never coming back. I realised the weight was gone forever and I had indeed found a cure for obesity that didn't lie in a pill, bottle, meal replacement, or even a rubber band. I had done it myself and it was permanent. Having that excess skin cut off was the most liberating experience of my life, more than being wolf whistled at or buying my first ever bikini. The daily reminder of the damage I had done to my body from years of self-abuse was gone, and I was free to live as the person I had set out to become—healthy, happy, fit and free.

Do what I did and you will lose weight. Replace bad habits with good ones and watch the fat just melt away. Eat well and often and see how great you look in a few months' time. Spend five minutes a day on the way you see and treat yourself and see how good you feel. Eat that elephant one five-minute bite at a time.

It doesn't happen overnight but it does happen. I did it and now it's your turn. I know you are probably waiting for the moment of inspiration to come to you. What if that moment, that desire to transform and save your life comes in the form of a heart attack or stroke? There is nothing motivating about being a dribbling wheelchair-bound vegetable. I know that's harsh but sometimes you have to hear the truth.

Every fat person knows that 'one day' they will lose weight. It's just the 'when' bit they haven't quite figured out. Over the space of two weeks, I broke three chairs in situations each more embarrassing than the last. The first was at a barbeque, where I was eating my four sausages and half a plate of potato salad (hoping no one would notice that was my second serving) and, in the blink of an eye, the chair just folded in on itself. Then, at the wedding of a friend of a friend, I gave new meaning to the words 'plus one'. Just as the best man was making his speech on the ghosts of girlfriends past, the legs of my chair seemed to melt, and on my way down to the perfectly polished parquet floor I managed to drag half the tablecloth, three plates of food and a beautiful, expensive flower arrangement down on my head. To make matters worse the best man then went on to save the moment (for everyone else) by saying, 'Well, she can't be accused of drinking on an empty stomach, maybe she's been drinking on an empty head!' Haha. Hilarious.

Three days after the wedding a restaurant chair did exactly the same thing. Every eye was on me while the waiter tried to make me feel better by explaining the chairs were cheap and not very strong. Cheque please! But not without two serves of dessert first.

Finally, with an already wounded ego but ever-growing stomach, I went to buy lunch from my favourite pie shop (funny how I had a favourite pie shop) and was asked whose baby I was holding. Surprised by the question, I told the woman who had served me the last nine months that he was mine. The sales assistant, as she handed me my two pies, sausage roll and cream pie (it was snack time) said, "Wow, I didn't realise you were pregnant." Pause… crickets chirping…uncomfortable silence…hasty and humiliating exit…quickly followed by three chocolate bars, a packet of crisps, two hot chip sandwiches and an entire cheesecake. I wish I could say that was the very moment I changed my life but it wasn't. Always been a perfectionist and I took fat as far as I could.

At the height of my eating disorder, I was approached by a film crew doing a documentary called *The Fat Trap*, wanting to interview me because I was obese. I had been running around the world claiming to be a goddess—all big and beautiful—but the word 'obese', and the fact that they had used it on me, shocked me to the core—my deep, morbidly obese, life-threatening core. Deep down inside, somewhere past the burgers and fries, I finally (and thankfully) heard the message. I was a single mother slowly killing myself. I was having heart palpitations, my blood pressure was so high I was on medication and I could not lie on the beach without Greenpeace trying to push me back out to sea. And all the time I was saying I loved myself the way I was, that the world had to change and not judge me for being big.

The truth of the matter is this: it was great that I loved myself no matter what size I was but to be proud of ill health is just wrong. Obesity can and will kill you, and if you truly think you are happy being a heart attack waiting to happen you are a big FAT liar, just as I was. The truth hurts but so does hiding from it.

And so I set out to conquer my demons once and for all. I was going to lose weight and get happy the healthy way (or healthy the happy way). I wanted to do this forever, not just for now or "by Saturday" or for my high school reunion. The change had to be permanent, and I was prepared to do whatever it took, for however long it took, to make it work.

In the beginning I enlisted the help of a shrink I called Dr Nutcase, a nutritionist I called Beansprout and a trainer I called Crusher. I became the ultimate human guinea pig. I did everything that was asked of me, tried everything on for size (pardon the pun) and read every book. I asked every fit, healthy or happy person I met a million questions, got a million different answers and tried a million different ways to live a better life. Not all of the techniques were for me but I was always learning and adapting. I had no idea if I was going to be successful but I had to give it one really good try.

I set up a camera up in my house and recorded most of my first year of getting healthy. I lost more than 30 kilos and did not expect in a million years the crazy roller coaster ride that was to follow.

At first, I filmed my weight loss as a way to make sure I wouldn't back out like I had every other time. For the first time in my life I had to really look at myself and listen to my own bullshit, and realised I was more tired of that than I was of being overweight.

'I lost more than 30 kilos and did not expect in a million years the crazy roller coaster ride that was to follow.'

Little did I know where that path would take me. There are days when I pinch myself and ask, "How did this happen?" Let me tell you, this was not the way I planned my life! Being called a diet queen or health and fitness guru still does not sit well with me. I was just a fat girl who set out to save her life and did.

The diary I kept of that first year became an international best seller called *Confessions of a Reformed Dieter*. Had I realised so many people would read it, I may not have admitted to such crimes as eating two entire pizzas covered in ranch sauce in one sitting, or getting so big

I had trouble wiping my butt. Oh, the shame! At the same time it was completely liberating. Reading about 'that girl', when I was no longer like that, made me proud of how far I had come.

Soon after my first book came out, I found myself on the talk show and public speaking circuit as an advocate for healthy weight loss and as an ambassador for the Eating Disorders Foundation. I was desperate to help others save their lives before it was too late. I set up my support website, www.healthybodyclub.com.au, because there seemed to be so many other women who felt isolated in their battles to love and care for themselves. To this day I do anything I can to keep that network going.

I was a single mum learning how to maintain my new healthy weight and lifestyle, while trying to raise a son with an (at the time undiagnosed) autism spectrum disorder known as Asperger's Syndrome. Boy, was life interesting (a nice way of saying 'pure chaos'). Over the next few years I sought a diagnosis for my son, continued to champion women's health issues, tried to raise funding and publicity for my support network, persisted with my own therapy, got engaged twice, broke up twice and wrote a kids' book about believing in yourself despite your size (*Blubberguts*). I responded to thousands of letters from readers of my first book, either thanking me for saving their lives, asking if I would become a personal trainer, or requesting that I write a second book explaining exactly what I had done to lose weight. This became *The Lazy Girl's Guide to Losing Weight and Getting Fit*, which like all of my 'diet' books is really an 'anti-diet' book.

Then one day the strangest thing happened: a message was left on my phone asking if I would consider hosting *The Biggest Loser*. I actually thought it was one of my friends playing a practical joke and so I ignored the call for three days. After repeated attempts to contact me, the producers reached out via my literary agent to see if I would come and meet them.

After confirming it was not a big fat joke I went along to a screen test. Seven days later I stood outside what was to become known as "The White House" and  welcomed the first group of *Biggest Loser* contestants. They all hoped to do what I had already just done: permanently overcome obesity and save their lives. I was the perfect person for the job—or so I thought.

I truly believed I would finally be able to reach out to and help those who had almost given up on themselves. At last people could hear my story and know how I had struggled to overcome obesity. I wanted to use my new found fame to send a message of hope and truth in an industry that seemed intent on selling people lies. Little did I know what I was getting myself into.

I am truly thankful for my time on *The Biggest Loser* but it was definitely not the glamorous life most people think. I should have known something was up when, a few days before filming, the stylist mentioned that it would be hard to get clothes for me because I was not small enough. Excuse me? I had just lost more than half of myself and was wearing size 10 skirts. The stylist explained that 'most hosts' were a size 6 or 8 and could therefore wear designer's sample sizes, making it easier and cheaper for networks to dress their talent.

Not long after the show aired, magazines and websites went wild with fat bashing—not of the contestants but of me. People wrote calling me a hypocrite who was 'not thin enough' to tell the contestants what to do. Few people who watched the show knew my story or that I too had recently battled obesity, and some of the things that were said about me broke my heart.

Add to that the challenges of being a mum, working 15- to 20-hour days, finding time to exercise and trying to eat well when the food on set was far from healthy (another irony that was not so delicious), to say I was doing it tough is an understatement. Maintaining health in everyday life is hard enough with adding all those pressures into the mix. My agent called and told me to lose weight, while magazines and radio hosts made fat jokes to my face. My weight was only fluctuating by about 5 kilos but by the reaction of the media, viewers and powers that be, you would think it was 50.

My first ever Logies were not as magical as I had imagined. I had a horrendous fitting with a very famous female designer, where her assistant looked me up and down and announced that Miss Hooty Tooty didn't, couldn't and wouldn't ever have anything in stock big enough to fit me. I was a healthy and fit size 12. A famous male designer then looked me in the eye and told me that in model terms I was a size 400. What is a normal girl from a normal world supposed to do with that? He's not so skinny himself. Maybe he was afraid my fat cells would rub off on his Botoxed balding head.

It soon became obvious that no designers would dress me. The network would have to buy a dress in, God forbid, a normal size from a normal shop. Oh the horror and shame of it all.

I found a beautiful dress (I love Lisa Ho for making dresses for normal women) but at the wardrobe fitting I discovered it had been bought a size smaller than the one I had tried on in the shop.

About an hour after the fitting, I received a text message from the head-on-a-stick stylist with the inspiring instruction, 'Nil by Mouth'. Funny. I'm surprised it wasn't followed with a Fed Exed packet of laxatives, a kilo of cocaine, and more supportive texts such as 'Eating is Cheating'. Everything I had fought for was being brought into question. I had had been hired because I was 'real', had lived the journey and overcome the odds, yet I was now pressured to become something I never wanted to be.

Four years later, I realised I had become a hypocrite of my own ideals. The pressure to be a stick insect was making me turn my back on all that I believed in. Sadly, the people who were supposed to be role models for health and fitness were anything but. I heard allegations of steroid use, excessive plastic surgery and nutrition "experts" recommending going without eating. I saw others chew and spit cookies into a bin, and received expert advice in the form of 'live off greens for a week, don't drink water for two whole days, dehydrate with pills and have half a glass of wine the day before a photo shoot to look the best you can'. Excuse my French but what the fuck?

These people are applauded for who they are (read, who they appear to be), while every time I turn around I am given grief for being normal. I never wanted to look like a supermodel or a body builder. I never claimed to be perfect or to know everything there is to know about weight loss. I was simply a normal girl who wanted to learn how to be healthy and not starve. I had found myself in a world where, just like Alice in Wonderland, nothing was as it appeared.

The demands to keep shrinking, long hours and emotional battle all took their toll on me. As soon as I returned to quick fixes and began to deprive myself, my weight became difficult to manage. I was once again seeking instant solutions versus everything I had learned and knew to be the truth: that slow, healthy weight loss is the only way.

In my fourth year of hosting the show, I was told that if I wanted to keep my job I had to go on a public diet. With every kilo I lost a sizeable donation would be made to an obesity-related charity. I had a son to support and not a lot of options at the time, but it very nearly killed me. After years of battling eating disorders the old demons were rearing their ugly heads. Those in power mentioned offhand that I might want to lose up to—and possibly even over—20 kilos. I was 70 kilos at the time. The only way I could reach that goal would be a starvation regime. I was at risk of becoming the very opposite of what I had fought to be.

Was I ever going to be thin enough to please everyone? Suddenly the recovered bulimic in me had a voice with power behind it. The power of the network, the power of the media, the power of whether or not I would ever work again.

I asked someone I trusted for help battling the eating disorder I had fought so hard against. Instead, I was screamed at by my agent for confiding in someone attached to the show and risking it getting out to the media. I had been extremely open in my healing and I didn't care if people knew. I just wanted to be healthy, not skinny, and certainly not at the cost of my life.

Many moments factored in to my decision to leave *The Biggest Loser* and this was most definitely one of them. I only just got through the final series without anorexia and bulimia taking over my life again. I wanted to go back to who I was—a normal girl who, after years of self-abuse, learned how to love herself enough to transform her life and become fit, happy, healthy and healed.

I forgot who I was for a little while. I got sucked into the belief that thinner and thinner makes you the ultimate winner. I stood on red carpets next to people who do three classes before breakfast, who only eat once a day, and who are convinced they are better than me and everyone else in the world just because they have 'bodies to die for' (read: bodies they might just die for). They want you to believe you must live a life of sacrifice to have the happiness you desire, wrapped up in a body that probably can't even reproduce because it is so deprived of nutrients. Just remember: not everything you see on TV and in magazines is 'real'. God knows I've been airbrushed enough times.

I have sat in Hollywood power lunches and watched, horrified, as women went to the bathroom seven times during a three-course meal. No job is worth subjecting your body to that. Not to me, and hopefully not to you either.

I am not alone in deciding I want a better life. So many people want to do the same but don't know how. That is my mission: to show you the way. I risked everything, packing up my bags and my beautiful son, and crossed the ocean in the hope of spreading this message (and perhaps getting Oprah's help!).

Here is the message with or without the Big O's blessing: you do NOT have to starve yourself to have a great body. Being thin does not make you a better person, more talented or more worthy. Guess what? Big girls get jobs, boyfriends and have a life too. So do medium-sized, short, tall, wide and round girls. What you get from life is what comes from within and you have to fill that with love, not food or hunger. Getting thin will not make you happy; getting happy will make you happy, and might just get you the body you want without torment. Being skinny and being healthy are not the same. You do NOT have to be a stick insect to find (and deserve) love and you do not have to go hungry to love yourself. All you need to do to transform your body and your life is to learn how to love yourself, regardless of your weight or size. Your goal is to strive at all times to be healthy and fit, and to treat yourself with kindness. That is when the greatest changes will occur.

I'm not telling you to be fat and happy. I'm saying be happy, then get healthy. When you are truly fulfilled, you will not seek food to fill you up. When you have suffered enough, you will no longer feel compelled to kill yourself in the gym. When you are ready to be happy, you will do whatever it takes to be so. My journey was more about transformation than it was about losing weight; that was just one byproduct of getting happy. Health, fitness, peace and wellbeing were the others. A richer, longer, more satisfying life was the best outcome of all.

'I'm not telling you to be fat and happy. I'm saying be happy, then get healthy.'

I might not be considered thin enough to be the perfect TV host but I say 'bah, humbug' to that! I am not just a survivor, I am a thriver. I'm taking the world by storm and you're all coming with me. I am a woman and mum who is no longer obese, who learnt how to turn her back on despair and taught herself how to be happy, healthy, lovable and loving. I am living an amazing life and revelling in all it serves up to me—including the bad days. Diamonds are formed under pressure and in every challenge lies a hidden gem that is yours for the taking. Be that precious gem, polish it until it shines and become all you can be.

I used to be the girl who drove down the end of my street to get a carton of milk. Just last year I completed a triathlon that had me swim, run and cycle a collective 31 kilometres. I did come last, but it was the first time I fully appreciated that the fat girl who had been eating herself to death would never inhabit me again. Obesity will never be that hungry wolf at my door—it is simply a distant memory, only visible in photos and the one fat skirt I still own to remind myself how far I have come. Next year I'm going to run a marathon and after that whatever I choose, because I can do anything I put my mind to and so can you. I have healed my life and continue to do so, and I can teach you to do the same.

Don't go looking in the fridge for answers—there is no wisdom to be had there. Don't drown your sorrows either because there is no love found at the bottom of an empty wine glass. (Yes, I know the more you drink the better they look, but it's not worth it.) If you seek to make a change for the better forever then come here, pick a page and devour that instead. Feeling down? Open to a page that speaks to you and let it lift you up. Struggling to get motivated? Come here, consider a new way of thinking and turn your dreams into a reality.

I read something great when I was 15: 'What we vividly imagine, ardently desire and enthusiastically act upon must inevitably come to pass.' Dream big; work hard; work even harder; and never give up. Just put one foot in front of the other and commit to making a thousand little changes—five minutes a week, a day, an hour. The more time passes, the more you will find your mind, body and life are better than you ever imagined. We are all time poor but we seek to be spirit rich, and this is the quick fix to end all quick fixes.

How do you eat that elephant? One small bite at a time. How do you fix your life? One small bite at a time. How do you get the body you want and the lifestyle to match? One little change, five minutes at a time.

Get stuck into this, one tiny, healthy, manageable bite at a time, and watch your heart grow, your life heal and your bottom shrink. The only way out is through, so start boldly, start strongly, just start now.

Put the chocolate bars down and Eat This!

See you at the beach!

x

# Getting
# Started

'The secret of getting ahead is getting started'

Agatha Christie

# KA-CHING

**What are you waiting for? To break a chair at your own wedding? To have your kids ask you to drop them a block from school so their friends don't see you? To lie contorted on the bathroom floor after having a stroke?**

It is not worth waiting for a magical ka-ching moment that suddenly fills you with the motivation you need. You will not wake up an entirely different person, healing a lifetime of unhealthy habits. It will take good old-fashioned hard work. No matter how shitty you feel, how far backwards you go, or how hard it gets, you need to pick yourself up and start again.

Having a healthy body is a lifelong commitment. It does not stop and start with a prescribed diet and a certain number of push-ups. It takes heart, courage and dedication to the idea that there is no end to the path: the ups and downs, highs and lows all contribute to one intention.

Your health is the puppy you got for Christmas: don't you dare give up on it or give it away. It's yours for life and you will not regret it. You have to believe that you deserve a better, healthier, longer life. You deserve to love and be loved. You deserve to treat yourself well. You deserve the very best of everything, right now. This is the time for you to save your life five minutes at a time, not when you are attached to tubes in a hospital bed.

# You've Got to Kiss a Lot of Frogs Before You Find Your Prince

One of the hardest concepts I had to accept was losing weight slowly. Previously I had gone for extreme, fast weight loss that I could never keep off. I had to adjust to losing, at most, 1 kilo a week if I wanted it to be healthy and permanent. You just have to let go of expectation and work on making changes instead of pressuring yourself to achieve everything in a week.

Let me tell you about the Green Frog Theory.

If you put a green frog in a pot of already boiling water it will jump out immediately, and thus be saved from a painful death. However, if the water is at room temperature and you bring it slowly to the boil, the frog won't register the heat until it is too late. Sorry froggy.

This is called the process of slow immersion.

Be gentle on yourself, expect success but not in the form of overnight miracles. Push yourself a little harder each day. Spend five minutes a day learning a new healthy living technique instead of missing five meals in the hope of fitting into a bikini by next week.

Don't expect too much of yourself or you will jump out of the hot water straight away. Immerse yourself slowly. You have the rest of your life to enjoy the changes so take the time to make them permanent.

# THE TRUTH

**Trawl through the Internet, spend any time in the diet section of a bookshop or speak to any fitness instructor and you will find a million different ways to lose weight. You will read for and against everything until your head (and hopefully your bum) explodes. There will be 'I lost my butt and found a boyfriend' poster girls for every extreme regime, no matter how wacky. The gadgets get stranger, the pills more powerful, the potions faster acting but none of them are capable of keeping you from returning to the habits that keep you trapped in an unhealthy body.**

Do you really want to spend the rest of your days picking the toppings off your pizza, having the equivalent of a gym in your living room, or behaving like some mad scientist at every meal—measuring, weighing and calculating every gram of protein and carbohydrate?

How many cave people do you think were on a diet? 'Thor honey, does my bum look big in this wildebeest pelt? Oh Blahthug, I really couldn't eat another freshly picked berry. Gee willikers, I will never get a husband unless I lose this unsightly cellulite that is so much more obvious than my unkempt underarm hair.' Diet products are a modern concoction for people with too much money and not enough self-esteem.

We, as human beings, are designed to eat a little bit of everything—not a lot of fat, not too little fat, not too few calories, not too many. We are not supposed to live as carnivores nor, with incisor teeth, are we meant to live like hamsters. We are supposed to move a reasonable amount (we did go hunting once upon a time), and we are meant to enjoy our time on this planet no matter how long, short, beautiful or ugly it is.

The list that follows is everything you need to know to lose weight and, if you stick with it, keep it off for the rest of your life. You will find that you read it and go, 'Der. I know all that already.' Of course you do. You already know all you need to lose weight whether you want to admit it or not. There is so much else going on with your head, habits and history that you have become convinced you can't do it on your own. I believe you can and will.

What I am asking you to do is put the diet books down, set up some new habits, throw out a few bad ones, love yourself and see how the body responds.

Let's get the simple stuff out of the way so you can focus on the bigger picture—healing your life so your body is a reflection of how good you feel.

- ✿ Women should aim at having around 1200–1400 calories a day. For a man, it's about 1600–1800 calories. You should aim to eat between 40 and 60 grams of fat per day (more for men). This is just a rough guide; don't live or die by it. Just live and don't diet!
- ✿ Stick to a breakfast, snack, lunch, snack, dinner, snack schedule.
- ✿ Eat every three hours or so. Don't eat two hours before bedtime (unless bedtime includes three hours of rigorous sexercise).
- ✿ Don't miss meals even if you are not hungry. Train your body to burn fat.
- ✿ Have three serves of fruit a day.
- ✿ Eat five different vegetables a day.
- ✿ Make sure you eat protein.
- ✿ Make sure you eat carbohydrates.
- ✿ Learn what healthy fats are and eat them—in the right portions.
- ✿ Have at least eight glasses of water a day.
- ✿ Take a multivitamin.
- ✿ Get lots of variety—boredom will send you to the fridge.
- ✿ Get lots of rest—particularly on days you have worked out.
- ✿ Do some form of exercise five to six days a week (even if it's just walking).
- ✿ Do your best.
- ✿ Do a bit better.
- ✿ Forgive yourself.
- ✿ Love yourself.
- ✿ Laugh often.
- ✿ Cry a little.
- ✿ Never give up.

# YOUR LIFE IS YOUR OWN BOOK TO WRITE

**Go out and buy a ring binder. Create your own workbook for your new healthy life. Decorate it and make it your own. Feel good about what you are going to put into it— both the work you do on yourself and the tools you use to create a better, healthier life. Fill it with goals, motivating pictures and quotes, recipes you love, food diary sheets, meal plans, worksheets, insights you learn about yourself, plans, mantras, quotes, inspiring stories of others—there are no rules, anything is possible. Your job now is to do whatever it takes to put yourself in the right head space to have a good day, a great week, a brilliant month and a fantastically amazing future.**

You life is an open book—you can write it however you like it. There is unlimited potential to learn, heal, grow, love and be successful.

Be the author of your own story and write like your life depends on it—it does!

# WARDROBE MALFUNCTION

**How many different dress sizes do you have in your closet? Most women have at least three, but if you had ballooned like I did your wardrobe would resemble a major department store. I had at least eight different dress sizes waiting for the day I could fit back into them—both ways. Why did I keep so many clothes? It was probably a combination of hope and fear.**

I had this gorgeous, long, black, size 10 velvet coat that had cost me a fortune. I loved it so much and I lent it to a friend on the proviso that she would give it back when I got skinny again.

One day I rang her up and asked for the jacket back. It was time! There was a long pause before she said, 'Oh, I never really believed you were ever going to lose that weight so I threw it out years ago.'

Why did I let my skinny clothes go, when I never did the same with bigger clothes? We all keep those pants or skirts for our 'fat days', while the skinny jeans get thrown out, given away or shoved down in the bottom of our closet.

By having a back-up plan you plan to 'go back up'. If you can easily dress yourself in two different sizes, you will continue to shift between them. If you throw the bigger size away, you will know it's time to eat a little less junk food and work out a little more as soon as your pants feel tight.

Go to your wardrobe right now and remove all the big clothes. Give them to charity, and give yourself the confidence that you will maintain your current weight and that you will never go back to being unhealthy.

# ARE YOU READY TO LOSE WEIGHT?

**We all have excuses to convince ourselves it's not our fault when the weight just won't budge . 'I've got big bones, my mother was heavy, I'm a single mother, I eat well, honestly I do…' Whatever!**

You will only lose weight when you are truly ready. You have to assess your life honestly to see if you can walk the walk as well as talk the talk.

It is often the smaller (and cheaper) decisions that get you to your goals sooner. Here is a hit list of changes you can make right now without picking up your credit card, guaranteed to have your butt a little bit smaller by next week.

If you can do just some of these, or even one a day, then you can work your way up to creating a full list of brand new habits and techniques that will transform your life and subsequently your body. Remember—to eat that elephant you have to do it one bite at a time, so open up and say, 'Ah'.

1.  Decide what you will and won't eat.

2.  Be proactive about everything.

3.  Make your home safe.

4.  Make your alternative (e.g. work or school) environment safe.

5.  Do big grocery shops and buy the right (fresh, healthy, low-fat) food.

6.  Keep your house junk–food free.

7.  Buy lots of fresh fruit a few times a week.

8.  Eat regularly.

9.  Eat as soon as you wake up.

10. Eat a good breakfast.

11. Don't eat too late at night.

12. Eat when you are hungry, not starving.

13. If you are starving, eat the healthiest food you can find.

14. Do not fantasise about food until you have a dream meal. Eat something healthy NOW.

15. Eat slowly.

16. Drink water before, during and after a meal.

17. Put your cutlery down between mouthfuls.

18. Sit down, preferably at a table, while you eat.

19. Never eat straight from the fridge or cupboard.

20. Keep your house well stocked with healthy, fresh food.

21. Be prepared for anything when you leave the house (how long you might be, where you might go, how many meals you might need to cover).

22. Never leave the house hungry.

23. Never shop for food when hungry.

24. Do not 'window shop' at food shops or food halls.

25. Plan what you will eat for the next week.

26. Plan what you will eat today and tomorrow (take food out of the freezer, make sure you have all ingredients, lay them out on the counter).

27. Plan for when you are pre-menstrual.

28. Plan for the weekend.

29. When you go to parties, take something healthy to contribute. Eat that.

30. Set realistic goals.

31. Set small goals.

32. Reward yourself.

33. Eat something yummy but healthy every day.

34. Throw away your fat clothes.

35. Do not rely on quick fixes: they don't 'fix' anything.

36. Drink plenty of water.

37. Keep water on you at all times.

38. Reduce salt.

39. Do not eat leftovers.

40. Do not eat while you cook.

41. Do not snack unless it is snack time.

42. Eat smaller portions.

43. Never have second helpings.

44. Never have three courses unless it's your wedding!

45. Reduce alcohol.

46. Reduce fat.

47. Reduce sugar.

48. Reduce carbohydrates.

49. Notice I said reduce, not eliminate. Eliminating anything makes you covet it.

50. Eat low-fat foods as often as possible.

51. Eat fresh fruit and vegetables as often as possible.

52. Buy low-fat, healthy recipe books.

53. Learn to cook your own food.

54. Cook your own food.

55. Do not skip meals.

56. Do not skip snacks.

57. Count fat (for now).

58. Count calories (for now).

59. Then stop counting cause you will have learnt to live a healthy life.

60. Realise that for every theory there is an equal and opposite one. Not all theories are good for you.

61. Do what works for YOU.

62. In the early days, try to eat at home as often as you can.

63. Cook healthy food for your family.

64. Exercise often.

65. Change your exercise regime so you don't get bored.

66. Exercise harder.

67. Exercise faster.

68. Push yourself.

69. Give yourself a break.

70. Try something new.

71. Timetable exercise into your life.

72. Realise exercise is not negotiable.

73. Realise eating healthily is not negotiable.

74. Do not overeat.

75. Do not undereat.

76. Stop making excuses.

77. Do not let others sabotage you.

78. Do not sabotage yourself.

79. Do not rely on willpower, it doesn't exist.

80. Get as much support as you can.

81. Do not be afraid to admit when you make mistakes.

82. Learn from your mistakes.

83. Do not be afraid to ask for help.

84. Be honest with yourself.

85. Stop blaming others.

86. Do not binge eat.

87. Do not binge drink.

88. Do not get drunk and order pizza (or strippers).

89. Plan social activities outside of meal times when you can.

90. Do not eat when you are feeling emotional.

91. Be strong.

92. Do not be afraid.

93. Get professional psychological help if you need it.

94. Realise that nothing is as scary as having a heart attack.

95. Realise you can do this.

96. Never give up.

97. Realise there are NO excuses.

98. Start now.

99. Start again.

100. NEVER SAY DIET!

# SIZE DENIAL

**I was once so fat you needed a train and two buses just to get on my good side. I didn't wear g-strings, I had the whole alphabet, and my belly button didn't have lint, it made sweaters.**

I might have been happy to make jokes about my size to anyone who would listen. I was also happy to show off my voluminous cleavage and say to all the skinny girls, 'you wish.' I was so busy calling myself a goddess, it was not until I was approached by a film crew doing a doco on obesity that it occurred to me: I was not only fat, but about as fat as anyone could get without actually killing themselves.

At the time, if you'd asked me what size I was I'd have lied. Absolutely blue in the face, through my teeth, crossed my fingers behind my back and walked myself to confession immediately afterwards. I would have told you I was a size 16 when in actual fact I was verging on a size 26. I was at the point where even kaftans were starting to feel too tight.

I would also bet money that I am not the first girl to do that. I have been mentoring and coaching women who wish to lose weight, and I guarantee most of them are a 'size 16'. They are all shocked when I quite frankly tell them they are kidding themselves.

The worst thing is, a lot of us are being fooled into thinking we have suddenly dropped a dress size or three. I'm sorry to be the one who tells you but your bum is not shrinking. Clothing sizes ARE getting bigger. Fashion houses are not stupid. They know you will buy anything that says you are a size 10 even if stripes don't suit and orange makes you look like you've eaten and subsequently vomited green eggs and ham down the front of your shirt.

The best thing you can do is get honest. Have a good long hard look at yourself. Don't be too harsh, just be real. Live healthily. Know that getting to a certain size won't necessarily make you happy: get happy first. Set yourself realistic goals. Don't try to overachieve but plan for a miracle: they do happen. And never give up—no matter how long it takes. Success is often the journey and not the destination.

# ACTION PLAN

**We've all experienced that horrible moment in the brightly lit changing room where you take in ten items and none of them fit. The Barbie doll sales assistant is glued to the other side of the door urging you to come out, and the last place you want to be is in the middle of a crowded store with half a leg squeezed into a pair of pants and a top that makes you look seven months pregnant.**

You skulk home and eat three brownies even though they won't help you fit into anything other than a mumu. You decide that tomorrow, being Monday and the hallowed 'day one' of all dieters, the diet fairy will suddenly visit and give you the strength you need.

Now we have the bullshit out of the way. It's time to realise it is YOU who needs to do the work—and the sooner you do, the sooner you can go back to that store and buy everything a size smaller.

Grab a pen and paper and answer these questions—they make up your five-step action plan. Acknowledging the truth of how you feel will give you the strength to see this to the end. I have put some sample responses here.

1.  **What are five reasons I want to change?**

    a.  I can't fit into any nice clothes.
    b.  I have no energy and don't want to go out any more.
    c.  I don't want to be like this next year.
    d.  I am so unhappy.
    e.  I don't try to do anything with my life because I hate it.

2.  **What are five reasons I need to change?**

    a.  I don't want to die young.
    b.  I don't want to have a stroke or diabetes.
    c.  I am not enjoying my life.

    d.  I am unhappy.

    e.  I deserve a better, healthier, more fulfilling life.

3.    **What five habits hold me back?**

    a.  I never plan my meals.

    b.  I eat too much chocolate.

    c.  I buy too much takeaway.

    d.  I drink too much alcohol.

    e.  I have a little success then give up.

4.    **What do I hate about being like this?**

    a.  I hate that I have so many clothes I can't fit into.

    b.  I hate feeling sluggish in the mornings.

    c.  I hate looking in the mirror and being depressed.

    d.  I hate that I don't bother to look good any more.

    e.  I hate that I am embarrassed when I see people who knew me when I was thinner.

5.    **What are five emotions I feel about myself right now?**

    a.  I am embarrassed.

    b.  I am sad.

    c.  I am repulsed.

    d.  I am disappointed.

    e.  I am angry.

**Now do these ones**

6.    **What five emotions do I want to feel?**

    a.  I want to feel happy.

b.   I want to feel sexy.

c.   I want to be full of energy and confidence.

d.   I want to love myself and my life.

e.   I want to wake up and be excited by my day.

7.   **What five habits I can fix first?**

a.   Plan my meals.

b.   Exercise.

c.   Change my chocolate bars for low-fat chocolate snacks.

d.   Stop buying takeaway.

e.   Cut down my drinking.

8.   **What five actions will I put in place today?**

a.   Eat a healthy breakfast.

b.   Eat a piece of fruit right now.

c.   Drink a glass of water right now.

d.   Make time to exercise.

e.   Remind myself what I hate right now and how I want to feel.

9.   **What five habits will I put in place this week?**

a.   Do a healthy food shop.

b.   Plan all my exercise sessions.

c.   Plan most of my meals and take lunches and snacks with me.

d.   Try on an item of clothing I really want to get back into.

e.   Make sure I have my water quota every day.

10.   **What five mantras can I say to myself to help me achieve my goals?**

a.   The only way out is through.

b. I deserve to be the very best I can be.

c. I am healthy, strong and immune.

d. 80 per cent of success is just showing up so go to the gym!

e. Progress not perfection!

**And finish up with these:**

11. What are five goals I can set AND achieve (be realistic)?

a. Lose 5 kilos or go down a dress size.

b. Lose 20 kilos by this time next year.

c. Plan at least five out of seven lunches and dinners for this week.

d. Exercise at least three times this week.

e. Join a sports team or do a fun run.

12. What five activities will I enjoy when I get to goal?

a. Shopping and buying a slinky red dress.

b. Sex (in or out of the sexy red dress).

c. Swimming in a bikini—book a trip to Thailand with the girls.

d. Bungee jumping.

e. Getting out of bed full of energy and loving myself.

13. What will feel the best about getting to my goal?

a. Fitting into my clothes.

b. Having energy.

c. Being happy.

d. Being healthy.

e. Feeling confident.

14. **What will be the five best outcomes of getting to goal?**

    a. Knowing I could do it and actually doing it.

    b. Rediscovering my entire wardrobe.

    c. Going into shops knowing there won't be tears.

    d. Saying yes to invitations without worrying about how I will look.

    e. Having the confidence to live my life fully.

15. **What five emotions will I feel when I get to goal?**

    a. Happy.

    b. Sexy.

    c. Confident.

    d. Loved.

    e. Fulfilled.

Now compare your answers from the first five questions with the last five. How much more incentive is there to get to your goal rather than stay where you are right now?

# GOAL SETTING

**Do you know the difference between millionaires and billionaires? Millionaires set goals once a day, billionaires twice.**

I don't know if that is true but I do know the value of goal setting. There really is no 'secret' to manifesting your dreams other than clearly knowing what they are, seeing what needs to be done, doing it and enjoying the rewards.

Write your goal down. It doesn't matter how you write it, where you write it, whether you write it in present tense, past tense, by hand or on toilet paper. Just be clear, focused and real.

For example:

*I, Ajay Rochester, am so happy to have sat on Oprah's couch some time in the year 2011. This is the first of many times I will be chatting with her on the subject of healing your life, as I have only just begun sending my message of hope to the world. I love continuing to run marathons after completing the first in March 2011 and my fit, toned, muscled but still sexy runner's body is a reflection of the time I put into my training. I love that I can divide my day up into time for Kai, me, my business, my running, helping others, being creative and pursuing my passions. I love being healthy. I love being fit. I love that Kai is settled, healthy, happy, flourishing in school and has friends and a life he adores, same with me. I love that I am a walking, talking, embodiment of good health while being real, raw and honest. Every day I wake up joyful for everything: the good times we bask in and the tough times that got us here. I love, am in love, am loved dearly and am truly happy, blessed and grateful. I completely respect my heart, my health, my friends, my family and all that I am.*

Easy, right? Now read it every day; change it whenever you want; write several more for the week and smaller ones each day. Keep working and reminding yourself where you are headed. Remember that you deserve the very best life can offer, and do not stop until you get whatever it is that you seek.

# GET REAL

**Answer these questions honestly**

1.  Am I ready to do whatever it takes to make my goal a reality?

    List the reasons you might not want to lose weight and get healthy.
    Now counter those with the reasons you do want to achieve this goal. If you write 'it is safe being fat', combat that with 'it's not safe to overeat'. For 'I can't cope with being a sexual being', think 'I will do self-defence classes and become strong'.
    Whenever you fall down, refer to both lists and focus your attention on the positive aspects of getting healthy instead of the negative.

2.  What may stop me from achieving my goals? Write solutions to these problems.

    E.g. I don't have time to exercise: I will mark time in my diary and make it a priority.
    I don't have enough money: I will give up takeway and use that money for gym membership.
    I have arthritis: I will swim and do aquarobics.

3.  What are my strengths?

    E.g. I am determined. I am brave. I am not afraid to try new things.

4.  What are my weaknesses and what can I do to overcome them?

    E.g. I give up easily: I will read my goals first thing every morning and do my best. I will get my best friend to ring me every week and give me a motivating talk.
    I love chocolate: I will use it as a reward and have only one chocolate a week.

5.  What are the ways I sabotage myself?

    E.g. Every time I lose weight I pig out. I put off exercise until I am too tired to do it.

6.  How will I prevent that from happening?

E.g. After weighing in I will be prepared with a low-fat treat such as Turkish delight. I will make sure I am busy on weigh-in day so I don't have time to sit and binge. I will not weigh myself for a month.

7.  Who supports me in my ideals? List everyone who can help you.

E.g. My mum babysits for me. My best friend gives me pep talks. My neighbour walks with me. My counsellor helps me heal.

Whenever you feel yourself crumble, actively seek the support you need. If you keep doing this, your success is guaranteed.

8.  Who sabotages my goals? Find ways to deal with them.

E.g. My mother-in-law always has unhealthy desserts at dinner: I will take a sexy fruit salad. My friends always bring junk food into my house: I will tell them it is no longer welcome.

9.  How can I make exercise more interesting?

Don't expect to have some kind of magical motivation. Find ways to trick yourself into exercising.

E.g. I will join a team sport. I will form an indoor soccer team with people who have never played.

10.  What do I really want?

Hopefully your goal is health and fitness. Losing weight will not solve all your problems, nor will it instantaneously make you happy. You need to work on getting happy first. Don't wait to lose weight before you start working on your dreams. Embrace and become your new self now. And if all else fails: bluff it until you become it.

Don't just read these and answer them in your head. Write them down, answer the questions and put them in your folder (you know, the one that is now overflowing with life-changing information). Answer them again in another month's time.

# Warning Signs

**Do you:**

- ✿ Always make sure you are the person taking the photos, or stand behind everyone so you can't be seen?
- ✿ Always 'sit it out' when you take your kids to the pool or beach?
- ✿ Avoid social situations because you 'have nothing to wear?'
- ✿ Get embarrassed when you meet people you haven't seen for a while?
- ✿ Avoid people you knew when you were thinner?
- ✿ Sit on the lounge with a pillow covering your stomach?
- ✿ Not play with your kids at the park?
- ✿ Have a list of activities you are going to do when you lose weight?
- ✿ Have pants that you cannot button up?
- ✿ Not attend reunions because of how you look?
- ✿ Have a cupboard full of clothes that don't fit you?

**If you said yes to any of these, stop and assess what is really going on. You blunder around denying that excess weight is affecting your life, but if you really consider what you say, think and do, you may be shocked at just how much being overweight is limiting you.**

Photos are taken to remember great times we have enjoyed with our family and friends. My mum was overweight and always took the photos instead of being in them. As a result, I have very few photos of her and I together, and when my son Kai asks about her I have nothing to show him.

I now take as many photos with my son as I can. We have albums overflowing with loving, silly and meaningful moments so much more precious than anything else in the world. It is a testament to our healthy, happy life—one we almost didn't have.

I used to hide in photos. Now I want them taken wherever we go.

I used to not fit in the swings at the park. Now I race my kid to the slide.

I never went to the beach at all, let alone got into the water. I now live at the beach and own ten bikinis.

I crossed the street when I saw people I used to know. Now I am catching up with all my old friends from high school.

I never went anywhere. Now the world is my oyster—I have recently moved to sunny LA where Kai and I are living the Hollywood dream.

Don't hide away. Don't limit your life because of how you feel about yourself. Don't get depressed about the way you are now, get excited that you are doing something about it. This Christmas you will stand proudly in the family photo instead of hiding behind the tree.

# Big Fat Lie

**Why do you insist on calling it 'pregnancy weight' despite it being years since you had a kid? Why not just call it 'the fat I put on when pregnant and refuse, for some reason or another, to take off'?**

I used this very excuse myself, and I have learnt to recognise the BS when I hear it. I don't say, 'Hmm I really can't shift this I-drink-too-much-alcohol weight.' Or, 'Gee I'm having a hard time losing these two-pizzas-a-week kilos.' Or even, 'I really want to get rid of this I'm-too-lazy-to-exercise spare tyre.'

Did you know that fat gets burned off the same way no matter how it happened to get there in the first place? My post-accident, post-pregnancy and post-fish-and-chip fat is all still fat.

The reason we label it 'pregnancy weight' is that it becomes an accepted smoke screen to hide behind. As soon as you say those words the heads nod, the sympathetic 'hm-hmm's fly around the room and you will immediately be given a list of reasons why you don't have to lose that weight yet—even if it's been five years.

Good food and exercise WILL shift the weight gained in pregnancy. No woman should submit to media-driven pressure to drop three dress sizes a week after giving birth, but don't use it as an excuse months or years later. It is hard having a child and exercising; I know because I live with the challenge every day. It is not impossible. Thousands of women find a way, with creches, sports strollers, exercise DVDs or by walking around their local park while the kids play on the swings.

If you want to lose the weight you must make the commitment to do whatever it takes. Then you need to get off your bum, go for a walk and remind yourself you are getting healthy, and post-pregnancy or not, you are taking back your body!

# THE SKINNY ON SKINNY JEANS

**Every girl has what she calls her 'skinny jeans'—the Holy Grail of her wardrobe. For you, it might also take the form of a dress, skirt, shirt or jacket. You either bought this much-loved item of clothing that almost fit, and convinced yourself that you would diet your way into it, or you did actually fit into it once upon a time and dream of 'one day' getting back there.**

Most people would say to throw it out with your other unfulfilled dreams. I say use it as inspiration. There is nothing like the cold hard reality of lying on the floor with the jeans only up to your knees to make you refocus your goals.

I find 'skinny jeans' a great way to assess your success without focusing on a number on the scales. With each new dress size I conquered, I went straight out and bought another item of clothing one size smaller, and tried it on once a week until it fitted.

Go and get your skinny on! When they fit (and they will), leave them on, ring up the girls and have an instantaneous night out on the town to celebrate!

# CHANGE THREE THINGS TODAY

**I'm not asking you to diet, go without, struggle or kill yourself in the gym. All I ask is that right now, you change three things you are going to do today and make them better choices. Not the best, or perfect, just better.**

For example, if you were going to go out to a long lunch with some work colleagues, then order and eat a salad before you go. Meet up with them towards the end of the meal, claiming work kept you back—saving approximately 1500 calories depending on how long your lunches are (and how many wines you can drink without going back to the office and photocopying your private parts).

Go soda-free just for today. Then commit to drinking your entire water intake and more. See how good you feel.

If you skipped breakfast to 'save yourself' for your long lunch (when in actual fact you were just training your body to store that food as fat), pop into a 7-11, grab a piece of fruit and yoghurt, and eat them now.

This exercise is all about seeing how you feel when you make small changes, while taking off the pressure to achieve certain results. Imagine if you did this every day. You could swap sleeping in on Sunday to hiking with friends. You could set your alarm one hour earlier and do a DVD workout without even having to leave your home. You could even decide on having an all-raw day (raw vegies), or no sugar, or do sit-ups instead of smoking cigarettes.

# Balance the Budget

**Losing and maintaining weight is a very simple equation. If you eat more calories than you burn off, your body will store the excess energy as fat. If you eat fewer calories than you burn off, your body will take fat as an available energy source.**

If you eat fewer calories than you actually require to function, however, your metabolism will go into starvation mode. It will store anything you eat as fat because it believes it has to 'save for a rainy day'. When you require energy, the first thing your body will 'eat' is muscle. For those who need it spelt out to them—your heart is a muscle!

With that information, you can easily live a balanced life. A quick assessment of your day can help you make decisions to keep you fit, healthy and light on your feet. Just remember this little ditty and you can never go wrong: heavy brekkie, light lunch, thinner dinner.

# Kick the Habit

**It takes 21 days to create a new habit, so why do you think that a few days of dieting will fix the rest of your life? Now that I have you thinking life changes instead of quick fixes, you can work on creating one permanent habit at a time.**

Let's tackle the first one together. You're going to find it silly at first but trust me—it works.

We're going to create the habit of slowing down at meal times. Studies have shown that overweight people tend to eat too much (no kidding), too fast. Follow these steps to turn that habit around.

- ✿ Prepare your food and present it on a plate.
- ✿ Pour yourself a glass of water or a cuppa to go with it.
- ✿ Turn the TV and music off.
- ✿ Sit at the dining table.
- ✿ Do not do anything else while you eat.
- ✿ Take one bite and put your cutlery or food down.
- ✿ Take your hands OFF your food.
- ✿ Now I want you to chew as if you have been put on slow motion. Really slowly.
- ✿ Focus on how good the food tastes and feels.
- ✿ Focus on how healthy it is.
- ✿ Feel it nourishing your body.
- ✿ Feel it energising you.
- ✿ Swallow it and really enjoy the sensation of fuelling your body.
- ✿ Have a sip of water.
- ✿ Start again.
- ✿ Repeat the steps above.
- ✿ As soon as you feel full stop eating.
- ✿ Drink some water.
- ✿ Do not eat any more until you feel hungry again.

- ❀ When you feel full again stop eating.
- ❀ Throw the rest away (or freeze it for another time).
- ❀ Drink some more water.
- ❀ Notice whether you have an automated response to eating. Do you immediately wonder what sweets you can have?
- ❀ If so, remind yourself that you have had enough to eat.
- ❀ If you really 'need' something sweet have a piece of fruit or some yoghurt. No lollies, no ice cream, no cake. The dessert mentality is a learned response and a habit you can tackle next week.
- ❀ Congratulate yourself and know that soon you will eat less and still feel satisfied.

Try another one: eating a daily quota of fruit.

- ❀ Buy some fresh fruit. Ensure you always have some on hand—and rotting bananas for banana bread do not count.
- ❀ Restock through the week so you don't run out.
- ❀ Buy a good range: apples, strawberries, blueberries, kiwi fruit, bananas, grapes and oranges.
- ❀ At snack time, try to have a piece of fruit instead of, for example, a chocolate muffin. If you substitute just one of your less healthy daily snacks with fruit you will make a difference.
- ❀ Ensure you always have fruit in your handbag when you walk out the door.
- ❀ Replace lollies and chocolate with a fresh fruit salad and yoghurt.
- ❀ If you feel you must have lollies or chocolate, apply the 'fruit first' rule. Perhaps by the time you've eaten the fruit you won't want another snack.
- ❀ Keep a fruit bowl at work or by your desk, preferably closer than the charity chocolate box.
- ❀ Keep a sturdy piece of fruit in the glove box of your car to combat hunger before heading to the shops.

You have created another habit for life. Now you are ready to tackle the next one on your list. Good luck!

# FOOD FRIENDS

**I have had many friendships that I based around food. Basically we would get together and eat crap, feeling safe in doing it with someone else. We would have a bit of a giggle over the not-so-healthy meal we were eating, then we would whinge and moan at the size of our bums.**

One day I decided that I would no longer catch up with friends over meals. Instead, we started walking together and going to dance classes. When we do eat we encourage each other to have healthy food. We made a pact that for the last few years has worked wonders.

I have become very discriminating when choosing potential relationships; I cannot be with someone who has an unhealthy lifestyle. It's like a reformed alcoholic living with a binge drinker or a cleaned-up heroin addict marrying a junkie. This will shock many people, but I will not under any circumstances date someone who lives off junk food and takeout. That just doesn't work for me anymore. I need someone committed to fitness and dedicated to living a long, healthy, happy life free from addictive and destructive behaviours.

If you have someone in your life who keeps you trapped in the body you have, you need to get serious about dealing with it. You don't have to make a fuss or even tell them that you want to change, just start suggesting alternative things to do.

Change your food friends to workout mates and you will get to goal so much faster!

# PHOTO FINISH

**I like to carry a fat photo with me to remind me of my goal. After years and years of overeating, laziness, self-sabotage, self-abuse, emotional attachment to food, bad habits and excuses, I made a commitment to never go back there again. There are times in my life when it is easier than others. Change does not happen overnight and you are always learning.**

When it is tough, I simply return to everything I have learnt, and every now and then I use my fat photo to remind myself of how it felt to be ticking-time-bomb heart-attack candidate.

When I was losing weight I had two photos on my fridge. One was the worst, fattest photo I could find of myself, and the other was a younger, fitter one that reminded me what I had been before and could be again.

Sticking those photos on the treadmill makes me run away from the old me and towards the new me. Having them in my bag when contemplating food I don't need makes it so much easier to remember how easily I could choose one path over another, and then the choice is easy. Health over heart attack any day please.

# The A-Z of Weight Loss

**Here's something quick and fun that can help you refocus. Every car needs a grease and oil change every few thousand kilometres and so do you.**

List the A-Z of what you can and are going to do to get to your goal.

For example:

**A** Accept responsibility.

**B** Be prepared whenever I leave the house.

**C** Calorie control.

**D** Drink lots of water.

**E** Exercise six days of the week.

**F** Fat—only eat good fats and avoid the bad ones.

**G** Grains—eat bread with wholegrains.

**H** Healthy mind = healthy body. Go to therapy.

**I** I am the one that makes it happen.

**J** Just say NO!

**K** Keep going no matter what.

**L** Love myself.

**M** Move it to lose it.

**N** No alcohol (sigh).

**O** Open my heart—look for the real reasons I do not let myself achieve my goals.

**P** Plan all my meals.

**Q** Quit looking for excuses to not do something, look for reasons to do it.

**R** Read inspiring books.

**S** Soccer! Love it

**T** Take control. Train.

**U** Up the ante. Work harder and faster every time I hit the treadmill.

**V** Vitamins.

**W** Weights. Do them. Go to pump class.

**X** Xcitement at reaching my goals.

**Y** You need to never, ever, ever give up no matter how tough some days are.

**Z** Zzzzzzzzz—Rest and recover.

It doesn't really matter what you write, and you can do this every week if you want to. The key is to go down the list and see if you are actually making the changes to your lifestyle. If not then shake it up, do what needs to be done and get on with living a healthier life and a hotter body to boot.

# PAY THE PENALTY

**Be accountable for your goals. Set them weekly and monthly and write them down. Make sure they are realistic and achievable, but also ambitious.**

If you achieve your goals at the end of the month then well done! The reward is a longer, happier, healthier life. However, if you have not achieved a number of your goals then you will have to 'pay the price'. I can say your thighs will bloat, your belly sag and your pants not fit, but you've become accustomed to those things already.

Instead of buying bigger pants or burying yourself in a pizza you must pay it forward. You have to donate either time or money to a charity of your choice. Go and work at your local soup kitchen (that will change your relationship with food) or make a donation to the hungry kids in the multiple countries that need help.

Turn a vicious circle into something good while reminding yourself of your healthy body goals.

# Recognise, Challenge and Distract

**I truly believe it is what is going on inside of you that affects how you look on the outside. The best way to improve is by having a filter on what you are thinking, feeling and doing at all times.**

This process is called: Recognise, Challenge, Distract.

**Recognise the bad behaviour.**
**Challenge it with a new positive thought process.**
**Distract with a new healthy response.**

Recognising bad behaviour is the first step in retraining the way you live. So many people live in a state of virtual unconsciousness that just taking note of what you are doing can be enlightening, and sometimes a little frightening. You might recognise anything from bad habits to emotional attachments. Simply observing what you are doing, why you are doing it and how it makes you feel can really set you free—and that's just step one.

The next step is challenging this with a positive, healthy thought process. For example, you might stare inside the fridge out of boredom, or because you are seeking comfort. Challenge this behaviour with the knowledge that there is nothing comfortable about not getting into your clothes or having a heart attack.

Once you have challenged, it is time to distract. You caught yourself looking in the fridge for Prince or Princess Charming and you have challenged that behaviour with the knowledge that you won't find what you are looking for in there. Now go for a walk, phone a friend, do something nice for your neighbour, have a cup of tea, go and spend five minutes doing something nice for yourself. Whatever it is, make sure it is not what you were about to do.

And while you high-five yourself for avoiding the first of many pitfalls, remind yourself how amazing and clever you are and taste the success you have just handed yourself on a fat-free platter.

# SAVE YOURSELF RIGHT NOW!

**What happens when you spin out of control? You have to reach out, stop falling, grab whatever you can and drag yourself back. It's never too late but you have to save yourself now!**

If you practise being healthy for long enough, eventually the spin-outs get shorter and you remember they do nothing for you in the long run.

In the meantime, turn to the 'save yourself' list. This list is designed to pull you up out of the deep dark hole that seems to be dragging you down, and guides you back into the happy place.

The list can be different for everyone, but let me share what I do to pull myself up out of the downward spiral.

1.  I decide I am not going to wait for a dreaded ka-ching moment (when absolutely nothing fits).

2.  I make a list of all the people who can help me out of this—friends, trainers, family, etc.

3.  I sit down and pencil in some serious training sessions. I plan my exercise for the next four weeks and nothing gets in the way of those appointments—everything else gets organised around them.

4.  I try on my tightest pair of pants. I will not stop until they are loose again.

5.  I do a big healthy shop.

6.  I check and recheck that my house is 'safe'.

7.  I take the wine out of the fridge.

8.  I throw the vodka away.

9.  I sit down and reassess my goals.

10. I sit down and look at what dates are coming up that would inspire me.

11.   I scrounge around my house and find all the things I need to do to look after myself. I get my creams, cleansers, hair treatments, pumice stone, hand cream etc. I put them all in one place and make sure I use them morning and night.

12.   I plan all my meals and make a big salad for dinner, with enough for lunch the next day.

13.   I never leave the house without planning and preparation.

14.   I sit down and set dates to do fun things with friends.

15.   I make time for me—something I never do.

16.   I make an effort to do my make-up every time I leave the house.

17.   I say yes to every social occasion despite wanting to curl up in my bed and run away from everything.

18.   I give myself a quick reminder of all the great healthy things I can eat instead of comfort foods, for example, low-fat fudge brownies and marshmallows.

19.   I book a hair appointment.

20.   I book dinner with friends.

21.   I pull out as many inspiring books as I can find and start reading.

What you have to do is pick yourself up, shake yourself until you wake up and love yourself until you respond. Don't wait to fall apart so much that it is only despair or, even worse, a medical condition that makes you change. Reach out, plan, attack, plan some more and take baby steps out of the darkness and into the light.

# SIMPLE TIPS FOR HEALTHY LIVING

**Spend five minutes and assess if you are doing all you can to have as good a week as possible. Make the changes you need to make. It's not rocket science.**

1.  Buy fresh fruit at least twice a week.

2.  Drink plenty of water and carry a bottle you constantly refill.

3.  Carry plenty of healthy snacks when you leave the house.

4.  Be prepared for everything when you walk out the front door.

5.  Plan, plan and plan again.

6.  When you crave something sweet eat fruit, even if this means eating fruit and something else. Eventually the fruit will be enough.

7.  Make your home a healthy food haven and avoid buying foods that tempt you.

8.  Drink water with every meal.

9.  Stop eating before you are full.

10. Under-serve yourself at dinner. If you are still hungry eat fruit.

# THE PLEDGE

**I want you to take the pledge that I took ten years ago. Every time I fell face first into a pizza box, I picked myself up, dusted the crumbs from my mouth, stood tall and said this over and over until I finally made it happen:**

*I commit to being the very best that I can be. I deserve to love, be loved and most importantly, to love myself. I deserve a healthy body and I will never give up on myself, no matter what happens, and I promise to do whatever it takes to make it happen. Today is the first day of the rest of my life.*

Then I just got on with the job of being healthy. When I thought I had gone 'off track' I realised it was all one track—good and bad. Knowing that made it easier to start over, because it was all one journey with ups and downs.

Good luck with your own journey. Now that you've said goodbye to your old life there is no end to this one. It's called getting healthy and the more you put into it the more you get out of it. Easy.

# You Are What You Eat

*To change one's life, start immediately, do it flamboyantly, no exceptions.*
*Act as if what you do makes a difference. It does.*

William James

# The Breakfast Challenge

**When I was obese I never ate breakfast and rarely felt hungry in the morning. My first meal was usually past midday, and more often than not I ate to satisfy cravings instead of fuelling my body for energy.**

One of the hardest concepts to grasp is that most people have to eat more (healthy food) and eat more often (six small meals a day) in order to lose weight. Once you get into this habit you can actually feel your body burning fat. These days I can almost tell time by when I get hungry.

The best thing you can do for your body is eat breakfast as early as you can every day. Think of it as fuelling a car: the more you have the further and faster you will go.

But don't think I don't hear you! When you wake up the thought of food makes you feel sick, right? Do you realise this is just a habit that suits the way you choose to live?

You, as a human being, have an incredible ability to evolve, so pick your knuckles up from the floor, stop moaning about how you can't lose weight and try something that works.

This is how you do it.

Force yourself to eat something—anything—within half an hour of waking, even if it is half a muesli bar or a breakfast smoothie. Start with a single grape if you must. After a few days you WILL start to wake up hungry. Within a week or two, especially after adding exercise to the mix, you will wake up starving and will have no trouble eating a protein-rich egg on toast.

Welcome to the world of being a lean, mean, fat-burning machine. Getting hungry just before meal times means your metabolism is awake, and each time you fuel it you are giving your body permission to burn fat. The longer your metabolism works throughout the day (i.e. the earlier you wake it up) the more fat you burn. Simple. Burn baby burn. Light your fire!

# MEAL PLANNING

**When I decided to never be obese again I realised certain things needed to change, not least my complete inability to even boil water without blowing up the kettle (don't laugh, I really did that!).**

So the first task I set myself was to learn how to cook. I bought every low-fat recipe book I could find, asked healthy friends to show me what they ate and watched as many cooking shows as I could stand.

Every week, Kai and I sat down with my beautiful pink recipe folder, overflowing with recipes torn from the mags I scoured at the doctor's office. I would cough loudly to cover up the sound of tearing pages—a bit naughty, but when you find a recipe for low-fat cheesy tuna bake you simply must have it!

We planned five home-cooked meals and left two open for freezer meals, healthy takeout or dinner with friends. We also planned to use the leftovers for healthy lunches. If we had chicken breast the night before, Kai would go to school with chicken and salad sandwiches and I would have a low-fat chicken Caesar salad. We made a list of ingredients, transferred our chosen recipes into the smaller folder in the kitchen and bought our groceries without ever succumbing to impulse purchases.

These days I am a whiz in the kitchen (modest too!), and can usually turn anything fatty into a healthier meal.

# Everything Must Go

**Feeling inspired? Just watched *Rocky* for the one-hundredth time and feel like you can conquer the world? Can you hear the music? Can you see the stair run? Can you see your hot bod at the end of the journey? Can you feel the fitness coursing through your veins? Can you hear the wolf whistles? You're gonna do it this time, you know you are.**

You want to do everything, something, anything at all. You just want to start NOW.

Get up right now, do a couple of stretches and a couple of light jogs on the spot…you can hear the *Eye of the Tiger* beating in your heart!

Seize the moment. Take your destiny in your hands. Punch the air a few times. Roar!

Now walk into the kitchen, open the fridge and empty out all the crap that has been keeping you from your goals. Go to your cupboards and grab all the candy and chocolate bars you can find, all the high-fat packet pastas, all the chips and dips. Stuff them in your pants. You heard me: stick them in the legs of your pants. Do you see how lumpy they make your legs look? Throw it all in the bin.

Do the same anywhere else you might have food stashed. Chips, chocolate, lollies, biscuits—anything that is not fresh fruit and vegetables or healthy whole foods has to go. Don't even think about keeping the processed snacks 'for the kids' that you eat more than half of. Send them to school with an apple and a sandwich instead.

Throw it all away, and while you are at it, go and get your biggest pair of jeans, the ones that are already way too tight. Cut them up, burn them and toss them out. Grab a fat photo and cut that up too. Say goodbye to the out-of-control emotional eater and say hello to the dedicated health and fitness freak you are becoming.

# ELECTRIC SHOCK THERAPY

**I was once invited to do a crazy stunt on breakfast radio to promote** *The Biggest Loser*. **The hosts thought they would turn the tables and put me in the hot seat for once—quite literally. They strapped me into an electric chair and proceeded to quiz me on the specific calorie content of a range of foods. Every time I answered incorrectly I would get an electric shock.**

The funny thing was, I had become what could only be described as the Rainman of calories. I knew the exact calorie difference between a cheese and pepperoni pizza, how many were in a Krispy Kreme doughnut versus a cinnamon one, daily requirements for men and women (with and without exercise) and so on. The shocked silence of the radio jocks as they saw their on-air stunt fall flat was pure gold.

My last answer was only seven calories off but they decided it was enough to flip the switch. I screamed, they got what they wanted and I walked out of there feeling pretty darn good about how clever I'd become. Not bad for a girl who used to think fruit and nut chocolate was a healthy breakfast choice.

Years earlier, I realised I needed to know exactly what I was eating. I studied a calorie counter book like I was taking an exam. At first I just looked up what I was about to eat, then I looked up my all-time favourite foods (they weren't so favoured after I found out how long it would take to burn them off). Before dining out I would look up the best meal I could choose from the menu.

I looked up my groceries as well because labels can be deceptive. 'Low-fat' food is sometimes high in sugar, and 'no added sugar' can be a smokescreen for something that is naturally high in sucrose. Remember, those labels are there to sell you a product, not hold your hand when the doctor tells you the results of your cholesterol test.

This became a lifelong tool—I always knew what was going in my body. Believe me, even if you don't know how much fat is in a piece of cheesecake it will still end up on your thighs.

Of course, you shouldn't spend the rest of your life measuring, weighing and calculating everything you eat, but once you have that knowledge you keep it forever.

# When Tom Comes to Visit

**Tom (Time of the Month) comes to visit once a month every month, every year for the majority of your life. If you are anything like me, you become a sweet-eating, carbohydrate-craving, chocolate-devouring monster three days before and the whole week of his visit. Imagine how much hard work you undo falling under Tom's spell every time.**

If you accept the power Tom has had over you, you must now exert power over Tom. There is one simple tool to taming him: preparation.

By knowing when Tom is due you can be armed and ready. Have great low-fat versions of the food you crave on hand. Chocolate protein bars, low-fat mousse, liquorice strips, sugar-free lollipops and gum can satisfy those urges without setting back your progress.

Take some pain relief just before it hits rather than after hours of suffering; despite what you tell yourself, four bars of chocolate cannot ease period pain.

Do your hair, put on some make-up and wear something that makes you feel sexy. If you are feeling down, then treat yourself to a movie with friends. If you feel bloated take something for it; there are some great natural remedies for fluid retention. Stay away from the scales, or anything else that makes you react negatively. If you look and feel good, you won't use junk food to make yourself feel good.

Plan your week and plan to succeed. Tom must not rule your life.

# Mood Food

**Keep a food diary over the next few days and monitor what you eat, how it makes you feel and how much energy you have afterwards. Note how full you felt and how hungry you were at your next meal. To make comparing entries easily, give each a number rating or little smiley faces.**

After a few days you may notice that certain types of foods put you in a better mood, fill you up and give you higher energy than others. When you've eaten slow, fatty or higher GI (glycaemic index) foods you may find your mood and energy goes down. When you eat fresh foods such as salads, fruits and proteins you may find your mood stays up, you have more energy and exercise is easier.

Once you prove to yourself how good certain foods make you feel, it is easier to convince yourself to take the healthy option next time.

# CONSCIOUS EATING—NEVER DIET AGAIN

**Put up your hand if you have ever sat at home alone and worked your way through two blocks of chocolate, a pizza, a packet of your favourite chips and a bottle of wine or two. Just me? You bunch of fibbers!**

I challenge you to record everything you eat in a day. If you're feeling really brave make it a week. It may no longer be a mystery as to why those jeans won't zip up.

It's amazing how much extra food you consume when you are not paying attention. It can start with that chocolate-coated nut bar you think is healthy, then that piece of cake you talked yourself into because it's the secretary's birthday. Your lunch was pretty healthy but there were those fundraising lollies at the front counter, drinks after work, kebabs after the drinks...

You'd be amazed how many times a day your hand goes to your mouth without counting the cost. Pay attention so you don't pay later! Becoming conscious of your food intake can drastically alter the way you live.

Here's your hit list to becoming a healthier, happier you without ever mentioning the 'D' word.

1.  Keep a food diary to work out exactly what you are eating and what you should be eating. Compare the two. Cry. Then be happy because knowledge is the key. Take it a step further and plan your next day's food intake, this time within your calorie count.

2.  Take responsibility. It's no accident you ate an entire packet of Tim Tams while drooling over Brad Pitt in Ocean's Twelve for the thirteenth time this week. Remember: the only person who can fix it is you. Don't ever sit with a full packet of food and think you can stop at just one. Take no more than you need and put the rest away (far, far away).

3.  If you have a problem (overeating, undereating, bingeing) then own up to it. Go to a counsellor; start an online journal; join a support group (see the back of this book to get three months' free membership to Healthy Body Club—now there's no excuse); or ring a friend before you come unstuck.

4.  Be honest. Pretending it didn't happen will not keep it from your hips.

5.  Never graze—and that includes nibbling on bits of your children's food, eating from open bowls of nuts and standing at the fridge for an all-you-can-eat buffet. Eat only what you need. Food is fuel, and any surplus will wind up on your body.

6.  Eat healthy foods in the right amounts. Do it consciously. Pay attention. Make a sandwich, sit down and eat it slowly. You are more likely to feel full if you focus on the ritual of nurturing yourself instead of seeking 'satisfaction' in a thousand tiny bites. What are you looking for?

7.  Watch what you eat and how you eat, enjoy your food and remember that losing weight is all about the maths: burn off more than you consume and you will have the body you want. It's as easy as one, two and stopping at three!

Good luck and don't forget to put your brain into gear before you open your mouth.

# TIME TO CUT THE FAT

**You don't have to live off pre-packaged calorie-and-fat-controlled meals the rest of your life. Some of the healthier heat-and-eat meals are a great way to get started if you have no idea what you are doing, and are also good to have in your freezer or pantry as a back-up. However, for long-term health you really need to be eating as much fresh food as possible. That means you will need to spend some time in the kitchen. Before you go all dreadlocks and alfalfa sprouts on me, why not make smaller changes you can actually live with.**

Here's a quick list of ways to lighten the load in the kitchen without having to go to the Cordon Bleu school of cooking:

- ✿ Choose lean meats (preferably organic, but we all have budgets so do what you can).
- ✿ When cooking chicken, go skin-free. Instead of trusting your willpower ask the butcher to remove it before you take the chicken home. Otherwise there is only one place that skin is going—straight from your mouth to your hips.
- ✿ Goodbye fry. Steam, stir-fry, grill, bake or 'dry' fry but there is NO need to deep-fry anything. Use non-stick pans, sprays, veggie stock, juice or water. These are all great alternatives that will actually make your food taste better.
- ✿ Do not keep big bottles of oil in your house. If you don't have it you can't use it.
- ✿ If you need to 'grease' a pan, a quick spray of cooking oil will do the trick.
- ✿ If you can't go without, use low-fat versions of cream, sour cream and butter or try low-fat condensed milk—a great substitute for fatty coconut milk.
- ✿ Use fresh herbs and spices to improve flavour.
- ✿ Water down pre-made sauces.
- ✿ Blot food with paper towels to remove excess fat.
- ✿ Fill your plate with salad—a full plate of low-fat food is much more satisfying than a pinch of fatty food.
- ✿ Make sure you have a grill plate that is tilted so the fat runs off. You will be surprised how much fat you find in the drip tray.

* Don't eat nuts from a jar, bowl or bag. Nuts are full of protein and 'good' fat but too many will blow your calorie budget. Know their 'value' and divide accordingly in zip-lock bags or little plastic containers.
* Use sugar substitutes and choose those made from real sugar (such as Splenda) over the totally artificial ones.
* If you do drink juice (and you should only have one a day if you do) then water it down.

If you make gradual changes they are much easier to sustain, just like collecting a thousand drips of water from a leaking tap can fill a bucket you can use to water your plants. Be the change you want to make, one drop at a time.

# WATER EQUALS WELL-NESS

**Water is vital for fat loss. You must have eight glasses a day, no less. Tea, coffee, soda, juice or even low-fat cordial, while containing water, do not count toward this daily quota.**

- ❀ Water flushes toxins from your body.
- ❀ Water stops you from eating when you don't need to (our brain misinterprets thirst for hunger).
- ❀ Water helps fill you up before a meal, ensuring you don't eat more than you need.
- ❀ When it is dehydrated, your body stores water ON your body, whereas if hydrated your body knows to let go of the excess.
- ❀ Water aids your kidneys in cleansing your internal organs. That means your liver can be left to do its job: converting fat into energy and burning it off your butt.
- ❀ Water hydrates the skin and leaves you looking younger without Botox...okay, I know I'm stretching it now.

You WILL lose weight more easily if you are hydrated. It only takes 21 days to create a habit that will last a lifetime so why not give it a go?

Firstly, stop buying bottled water. Buy a water filter for your tap and make a Sunday night water ritual. Collect all the water bottles you use over a week and refill them with freshly filtered water. Spread them out over your fridge, freezer, gym bag, by your bed, by the front door, at your desk. Every time you feel the need simply reach out and grab a drink.

Add up the money you have previously wasted on a free, natural resource. Be amazed at how much you will save over a year and go buy yourself a brand new, in-season Gucci handbag as a reward for being so good. Or you could donate what you would have spent per month towards the purchase of a well for a village where water is not so easily accessible. Not only do you hydrate yourself as much as you should, you are saving the planet by not churning through so many discarded bottles and you can give a life-saving resource to a village in need. Now buy yourself the Gucci handbag anyway for being such a good citizen of the planet.

# Return the Favour

**If someone gives you chocolates it doesn't mean you have to eat them. If that person handed you a card saying 'this will erase all your hard work, leave you feeling disappointed in yourself, and reintroduce negative habits', would you keep it?**

Why not give the chocolates to your kid's teacher, to the folks at your local retirement home, or the nurses at a hospital? Better still, give them to a patient who doesn't get many visitors, and spend some time chatting with them as well.

It's amazing how you can turn what could be a temptation into an opportunity to express gratitude for all that you have.

# BROKEN RECORD LANGUAGE

**Don't you hate it when you finally decide to have a healthy week, and the first dinner party you go to the host serves their homemade creamy, full-of-fat whatever-it-is that they made 'especially for you'?**

You politely decline, explaining you are avoiding too much of that kind of food. WRONG WAY! GO BACK! This is what happens next:

*Host: You don't need to go on a diet. You look great. Go on, have a piece.*
*You: No thanks, I just want to have a healthy week.*
*Host: But this is all natural, I made it myself! One piece is not going to hurt you. Please.*
*You: Thank you but I can't. I'm really trying to stick to this diet.*
*Host: Yeah, but look at me…I'm bigger than you and I'm having a piece—plus, it's my birthday.*
*You: Yes, but I had so much dinner. I really can't.*
*Host: There's always room for dessert…and I made it because you liked it so much last time.*
*You: Oh, well…okay, I will then. Thank you.*
*You eat it because you have been bullied into it. You made the right decision and then you let them talk you out of it.*

Alan Pease is an expert on what is called Talk (and Body) Language. When you want someone to listen to you, he recommends using something called Broken Record Language. It works a treat.

You state your case simply and you do not give free information. You then repeat the same answer every time they try a different angle of negotiation.For example:

*Host: Have some dessert, I baked it especially for you.*
*You: It looks delicious, and I totally appreciate it, but I have had enough food. Thank you.*

*Host: Everyone else is having some, why aren't you?*

*You: It really does look delicious, and I totally appreciate it, but I have had enough. Thank you.*

*Host: What's wrong? Are you on a diet or something?*

*You: No, I appreciate it, truly, but I have had enough. Thank you so much.*

*Host: Oh okay, suit yourself. Anyone else?*

I know it sounds a little silly. I do change the wording a little so I don't sound like a rude robot, but trust me, this works.

# FIVE MINUTE SNACK ATTACK

**To keep your metabolism working you need to snack between meals two to three times a day. If you are not prepared, however, you may find yourself eating too much—of the wrong things—at snack time.**

Take five minutes now to prepare some healthy snacks for the week. Make a beautiful fruit salad or diet jelly. Pour the jelly into portion-controlled plastic cups, dropping a plastic spoon in each so you can just grab and go. Make fruit smoothies and freeze them as healthy iceblocks. Cut a mango in half, put it in a ziplock bag and freeze it—it tastes just like gelato. If you have more than five minutes to spare, make some low-fat muffins, freeze them in separate bags and throw one in your handbag whenever you are running out the door.

A few minutes of planning can make all the difference between having a successful week and taking a few wrong turns. Having healthy snacks on hand reduces the risk of falling face first into temptation.

# LIFE IS SWEET ENOUGH

**Recently I did one tiny thing that made a huge change to my whole week: I made the momentous decision to go without sugar in my tea.**

No big deal, right? After all it only works out to be about 150 calories a day depending on how many cups you have.

Wrong! It is a big deal; it's about changing your mindset. Like chipping away at an ice sculpture, all the little changes you make will add up, helping you create the body you want.

# CHEERS!

**I love a drink or seven but let me tell you: the best and most consistent weight loss I ever achieved was when I gave up drinking. I remember the first time I chose healthy body goals over how many stringers I could Kahlua-kiss at midnight on New Year's Eve. I woke up energised on New Year's Day, excited by my investment in my health. I went for an early morning run, tripping over people sleeping on the beach. I felt so alive and healthy, and so close to achieving my goal I didn't feel as if I'd missed out on anything. In fact, I felt like I'd been missing the point for years.**

There are things you need to consider before cracking open the champers. Any alcohol is excess calories, and skipping dinner to make up for them will only get you dangerously drunk. You don't want to end up like I did: hungover and in a wheelchair with a broken leg two weeks into my diet.

Some alcoholic drinks, such as wine and champagne, are quite high in calories. Spirits such as vodka are low in carbs and low in calories (particularly if only drunk with soda water), but it is the quantity that makes the difference. One drink is okay, one bottle is bad.

Beer is high in carbs and experts say it can contribute to weight gain around the stomach area in particular, which might explain why so many of our Aussie beer-drinking blokes look eight months pregnant with no fat anywhere else on their body. And for the record: fat stored around your stomach area puts you at higher risk of heart disease than fat stored in other areas.

When you consume alcohol with food, the body recognises the alcohol as a toxin and burns it off first. The food you have eaten is burnt off last, or worse, left as excess calories later stored as fat.

And let's not forget those extra foods eaten after having a few drinks. Not only does alcohol increase your appetite, it weakens your resolve. I can't tell you just how many extra meals or snacks I don't even remember eating under the influence. I could probably feed a third world nation on my midnight drinking munchies.

Before you book yourself into Betty Ford, keep in mind many health experts recommend drinking a glass of red wine a day. My Hermitage Grange–drinking grandfather swears blind (or is that 'swears until he is blind drunk') that drinking red wine prevents cancer and heart disease.

The reality is, drinking too much is bad for you. Having a few may not kill you, but try to make better choices. Water your wine down with soda water; drink less; stop sooner and don't drink your way to a midnight binge. Cheers!

# Party Time

**Why is it that as soon as you decide to 'go on a diet', your inbox is suddenly overflowing with endless invitations to parties, dinner dates and celebrations?**

'Party food' is just that, and while it might be tempting, there is no need to eat all of it all the time. There will be many parties and the food will pretty much be the same everywhere you go, so remind yourself that passing it up this time does not mean passing it up forever. There may come a time when what's on the table means nothing to you, because you are so busy being the life of the party you no longer turn to the food for company. And if you put down the cake long enough to walk around the room you never know who you might meet.

The key is not to panic when faced with temptations. Have some great 'rules' to help you through, and you will find life has more to offer than what's lurking on the snack table.

1. Never go to a party hungry. Eat a healthy, fulfilling meal first.

2. Always take a plate with a healthy alternative (low-fat dip, carrot sticks, pretzels, low-fat dessert).

3. Never go out to dinner starving. Have a protein shake or snack before walking out the door, because otherwise you will be famished by the time you order and that does not bode well when choosing what to eat (bring on the ten-course degustation meal!).

4. Always drink lots of water—between drinks, before meals and in between mouthfuls.

5. Never stand near a table of food. Go and stand next to someone single and good-looking instead.

6. Always exercise the day you are going out.

7. Learn to say NO.

8. If going out for the day (to a school fete, staff picnic etc.) you don't NEED to eat the food they have there, which may not always be a very healthy choice. You can pack your own healthy lunch and snacks.

9. You don't need to eat three courses every time you eat out. Save that kind of excess for one-offs. You could just settle for a main and a bite of your partner's dessert. I rarely, if ever, order dessert but always order a spoon.

10. Never feel obliged to do anything you don't want to. Your goals are just that—yours. Own them and make them happen.

By making consistently healthy choices, the party season will pass without your having to speed dial the lipo clinic.

# HAVING TROUBLE MAKING HEALTHY CHOICES

**If you are like I was when I was obese, you have become accustomed to needing a certain type of food to make you feel full and satisfied.**

When I first started, I hated vegetables, salads and anything else healthy. These days, I love a good salad, I'm getting there with the veggies and I love food that fuels my body. I can't describe how it feels to see your bicep bulge when you reach for the salt.

Time and again I have said 'bluff it until you become it.' You have to think, feel, act, talk, walk and eat like a healthy person, even if you are not one. These new ways will become habits and you will eventually become that healthy person. I promise. It happened to me.

If you say you hate lettuce you will. If you say you don't eat salad, you won't. What you need to do is reprogram your internal dialogue. Start looking at lettuce and salad in a different way.

For example, this is what I say to myself trying to decide between prawn and mango salad and a trip to the fish and chip shop:

*Fish and chips will just make me miserable after I've eaten them. They will undo all the hard work I have done at the gym and it will make my next meal even harder because I will feel out of control. Salad is light, refreshing, healthy, fantastic for my body and will have me weighing a kilo less next week. The salad always fills me up, yet I feel so light after eating it.*

*I just love how in control I feel after eating my salad. I can't wait to get to it. I am so proud of myself for being in control. I am strong, healthy and achieving my dreams. Damn I'm good.*

I am not saying 'eat a salad every day and every night for six weeks.' You'll just crash and burn if you try. But do have a few 'light meals' during the week. Salads are great if you make them interesting. As I say to Kai, 'It's a new thing. You might like it!'

# TRY THIS ON FOR SIZE

**For the next three weeks, do your food shopping online. Plan your week and order accordingly. This way you avoid all the tempting impulse purchases you do not need. And the really good home shopping sites actually remember your order, so shopping each week becomes faster and easier.**

Imagine having NO emotional investment or decision to make. You won't stand there staring and dribbling at the Oreos trying to talk yourself out of buying them. You won't put that roast chicken in and out of your basket three times. You just log on to the web, click the mouse and your low-fat fresh food delivery is on its way. And now do a workout with the time you saved going to the supermarket.

Remember: a safe house makes it harder to sabotage your goals and time saved can be used to save yourself.

# Eating Cheesecake Does Not Count as One of Life's Goals

**What will your life look like when you get to your goal? I made this list when I was 'on the way down':**

*I will be popular.*

*I will go out dancing.*

*I will play sport.*

*I will have friends.*

*I will do fun things on the weekend.*

*I will go to auditions.*

*I will be successful.*

*I will chase my dreams.*

*I will fall in love.*

Can you tell me why you cannot possibly do anything on your list just because you are not at your ideal weight? Why do you think that, just because you are not there yet, it somehow makes you unworthy of living the life you desire?

Had I actually gone over my list and done some of those things sooner, I may well have put the cheesecake down and not ballooned to the size of three whole people.

You are capable of being just as great an actress if you are big as if you are small. You are completely welcome to go out and dance yourself stupid regardless of how many chocolate bars you ate last week. And sport is not exclusive to Barbie look-alikes.

You are only limited by your ability to believe in yourself. You can laugh, love, sing, play, dance and dream no matter what weight you are, and the sooner you listen to and follow your heart the sooner your body will respond.

# Get Smart

**Shhhhh, don't wake me…Brad Pitt is feeding me chocolate-coated strawberries…ooh, now it's Johnny Depp waving his Turkish delight under my nose while George Clooney is cooking up pancakes in maple syrup.**

I'm not sure which I crave more: Johnny, George and Brad or the chocolate, pancakes and Turkish delight. But those constant cravings, and giving in to them more than I should, are what stands between me and that bikini I bought two years ago.

Whether it's sweet or savoury, meat pies, bratwurst, cheesecake or chocolate that you turn to, you need to take a good hard long look at yourself, ask yourself if you truly want a better way of life, and simply do whatever it takes to stop succumbing to temptation.

You don't have to give up everything you like forever. Whatever it is you crave, there may be a simple yet satisfying solution that will help you achieve your goals much faster.

Assess the kinds of food you like, and instead of trying to deny them find healthy alternatives. There is no point eating foods you don't like or find boring and unsatisfying simply to lose weight, because you won't sustain it. What you have to do is make lifelong choices. You need to find foods that are healthy but that you enjoy as well.

Love pasta? Then find some great low-fat recipes, make up a big batch on the weekend and have it during the day at work rather than bulking up on carbs at night. Halve the amount of pasta and add some greens. Love hot chips? Make your own oven-baked wedges, wrap them up in paper and walk down to the park to eat them. Have a sweet tooth? Make your own low-fat, low-sugar apple pie—or better still, a yummy fruit salad with low-fat ice cream.

Take a little time and cook your own healthy versions of the foods you love or have something so similar it feels just as good.

# My Friend the Chocolate Cake

**The first thing I turn to when things go wrong is my dear old friend, food. I have survived far too many break-ups and knock-backs with the help of late-night chocolate fumblings in my bedroom.**

Most people turn to food for comfort. It's not all your fault: it started with those lovely old ladies in the supermarket who saw you having a tantrum, felt sorry for your mum and handed you a lollipop to make you happy. That was the moment that ruined your thighs forever.

Emotional eating is a learned response. 'If you're good you can have ice-cream,' we are told as children. The food we were never allowed to eat in abundance became the Holy Grail of happiness. When we feel lost, confused, depressed, disappointed or frustrated we look back to those flavours to fill the gap. The problem is none of these so-called comfort foods really do the job.

Everyone has their vices. Recognising your weakness, and understanding why you give in to it, is the first step you need to take towards a healthier, more productive life. Once you understand the factors that contribute to emotional eating, you can actively learn to self-nurture in more fulfilling ways.

The first step is to identify what you are really craving. Make a list of what you might actually be looking for (other than fifteen chocolate frogs dipped in whipped cream). It could be love, success, power, security, acceptance or friendship. Only by identifying how you really feel can you start fulfilling your needs.

Prepare an action plan. Work out how you can go about creating the life you desire. If you want success write 'apply for better job'. If you want more friends, write 'join a sports team and get to know my teammates'. If you want power go into politics. If you want love grab a friend and go speed dating.

Once you establish what you need to do to change your life, find a new way to nurture yourself. Work out what makes you feel good. My thing is having a bath with oil, candles, soft music, incense and a good book. Yours might be going for a walk, getting a pedicure or massage or simply playing with your kids.

My shrink, Dr Nutcase, calls it 'Recognise, Challenge and Distract'. You need to recognise that you turn to food when you could be doing something more positive. You need to challenge that behaviour with a new thought pattern (e.g. 'I don't eat that food any more'). Then you need to distract yourself with a nurturing activity.

I promise you will cut your emotional eating in half, if not stop it altogether. It might not be forever; I have been known to have the occasional pizza and the odd block of chocolate, but not often. When I do eat chocolate these days, it feels like a treat and not an ineffective substitute.

You deserve to honour and love yourself. Don't settle for anything less than the best and don't give up until you have the life you desire.

# HAMBURGLAR

**We've all seen it: one hot chip thrown into a flock of seagulls, each of them cawing and scratching to have a piece of it. Is that what you have become? How many times a day do you pick at your child or partner's food, swooping down the second you serve a peanut butter and jelly sandwich, three squares for them and one for you.**

Or maybe you eat what I call the chef's preparation degustation—the one where you make a meal but eat three quarters of it before it hits the table. A baked potato here (you have to check if it's crispy enough), a slice of lamb there (is it tender and juicy?), a scoop or three of the mousse you are making for dessert.

How many times do you hand a packet of lollies or crisps to your kids but wind up eating more than them? Kids take lollies out of a bag one at a time whereas you probably shove three or four in your mouth at once.

And what about the leftover fairy? The one who magically hoovers up anything left on your child's plate. Who cooked seven fish fingers in the first place, knowing your four-year-old would only eat two or three at the most?

You, my dear friend, have become a cat burglar…or should I say a fat burglar? If you had someone follow you around for a week bagging up all the little extras you thought you got away with, you would be horrified to do the math.

**Take a look at this list:**

|  | calories | fat (g) |
|---|---|---|
| Leftover peanut butter sandwich | 80 | 5 |
| 2 fish fingers | 130 | 5 |
| 3 cocktail frankfurts | 180 | 15 |
| 1 piece of brie (30g) | 90 | 9 |
| 1 slice barbecue Meatlover pizza | 225 | 12.5 |
| 30g roasted peanuts | 190 | 16 |
| 2 leftover chicken nuggets | 100 | 6 |
| 2 bites of chocolate bar | 120 | 5 |
| 1 chocolate biscuit | 100 | 5 |
| 2 bites of ice–cream cone | 35 | 2 |
| A few fries | 60 | 3 |
| Handful of crisps | 60 | 4 |
| 5 squares of chocolate | 160 | 9 |

Total excess calories headed straight for your thighs: 2430, which is just under two days' calories required for a female on a weight loss regime (1200–1400 calories per day is recommended).

Total amount of fat requiring liposuction: 96.5 grams, once again roughly two to three days of the recommended intake for weight loss (20–40 grams).

It's not unreasonable to think you might graze on that many tidbits over a week. If you add it up over a year it equals more 12,500 excess calories, which is the equivalent of 345 days of food—yes, that is two years worth of food eaten in just one.

# Are you Eating Enough?

**The main reason people do not stick to their 'diets' is because they are starving. Worse still, the body will NOT shed fat if it isn't getting enough food to fuel itself.**

How many women do you hear say 'I just can't shift the weight'? There may well be a perfectly good explanation for that. When you don't eat enough, you put your body into starvation mode and the first thing you eat will be turned into fat. You could well be turning your body into a fat-making machine.

Remember, you don't have to starve to lose weight. Don't miss your snacks, don't skip lunch, don't sleep through breakfast and don't skip dinner so you can have a few drinks (we all know where that ends up!).

Remember to fuel your body so you have the energy to exercise.

Remember to eat enough food so your body knows to burn fat.

Remember you should not be hungry all the time, just around meal and snack times.

Eat the right foods and you will almost always feel full and satisfied.

Make sure you eat enough.

Make sure you don't mistake hunger for thirst.

Make sure at all times you remind yourself that eating is not a crime, food is fuel and exercise will give you even more energy.

# How to Survive the Football Pig Out

**Are you one of those people who hosts the footy final at their place every year? Does it involve lots of beer and ordering ten boxes of pizza? Does it end with you in tears, saying you'd been good all week but you just couldn't sit there and eat a bowl of lettuce while everyone tucked into their favourite fat-filled pizza?**

A lot of these foods we eat on special occasions are about the traditions we have created for ourselves. You have to transform your tradition.

First of all, substitute real beer with diet ginger beer, or even full-strength for low-carb. You can still have one or two, but not the fifteen you are used to. When it comes time to get the pizza, heat up a healthy homemade version you made the day before (or grab a Weight Watchers one out of the freezer). Ask the pizza people if they would be so kind as to throw in one more empty box with your order.

When the pizzas arrive, slip your healthy homemade pizza out of the oven and into the box, hand the others around and sit down to watch the football with everyone else. No one need know you are even on a diet. You feel a part of the gang but you eat a pizza that is actually good for you.

# Pretty Flowers

**I was once a sucker for the food hall in shopping malls. There was a time when I would buy half a double chocolate mud cake and half a cheesecake from The Cheesecake Shop, put them in the fridge and eat straight from the box, leaving a spoon in the cake to make it easier to graze all week long.**

I loved cupcakes, chocolate cake, cookies, French pastries, vanilla slices…you name it, I had an insatiable appetite for it. But one day I decided to treat my 'sweet tooth' differently.

I stopped to think about why I was attracted to these foods. They are so pretty. They are usually bright in colour or beautifully decorated. They are small and therefore easy to convince myself I can have more than one. They are generally associated with celebrations (cakes) and sometimes even gifts (those cute little chocolates in a range of shapes).

Every time I couldn't squeeze into my jeans it was those little packets of loveliness that floated around my brain, forcing me to head to the gym for hours on end and restrict myself to lettuce 'til I turned a pale shade of green.

One day I decided to visualise all the pretty cakes and sweets as flowers. Every time I passed the decorated windows and cabinets I would admire the colours and remark to myself 'the flowers look lovely today'. And just like a beautiful bush of roses or a lovely bunch of flowers by your bedside, I could simply admire the sight and smell.

I would sometimes even go so far as to walk myself straight to the florist and buy 10 dollars worth of mixed flowers (usually admitting to the florist what I was doing and in turn getting more flowers for my buck). I would congratulate myself on honouring my body while enjoying the touch, sight and smell of something sweet that wouldn't kill me.

The more I did it the stronger I got. I could look, walk past and not even think about buying those foods. I didn't stare in like a kid looking in a toy shop a week before Christmas. I was no longer smitten.

I don't pine for them, I don't miss them and sure, I can enjoy a slice of cake occasionally, but more often than not I am the one not ordering dessert at dinner and don't feel like I'm missing out.

# PIGGY BANK

**One of the most surprising side effects of losing weight was having more money at my disposal. Being overweight or unhealthy can be quite costly; takeaway food, dining out, alcohol and pre-packaged snacks can put a strain on your bank account you may not even be aware of.**

Go through your credit card or bank statement and you will see just how expensive this kind of lifestyle can be. Choosing a homemade pizza over a home-delivered one can save you 20 dollars. By being proactive, you will save not only money but your life as well.

One of the keys to succeeding at permanent weight loss is fighting the feeling that you are giving everything up for a goal you can't yet enjoy. Turn that thought process around and invest in the end product: your sexy new self!

Visualise how good you are going to look and feel. You are going to want to celebrate in style, in a way that won't undo all your hard work. You are going to need a new wardrobe so why don't you go out and get one? Think Julia Roberts in *Pretty Woman*! Plan a day in your local shopping centre, or even better take your girlfriends to one of those factory outlets.

Every time you save money by making a healthy home-cooked version of your previously expensive fatty takeaway meal, put that money in a special 'New Me Spree' bank account or piggy bank.

If you want to go one step further you can give yourself a bonus for every kilo you lose. It's a great way to feel satisfied about making healthier choices, will get you to goal sooner and gives you something to look forward to other than a weight on a scale.

# Don't Crash and Burn!

**How many times have you joined that 'delivered to your door', pre-packaged food service, only to find that as each week goes by you eat less and less of their food and more and more of your own? Around the eight-week mark your freezer is overflowing with the uneaten food, the fruit is so rotten it resembles a modern art sculpture, you've put on at least 2 kilos and even the dog won't eat the portion-, carb- and calorie-controlled 'roast beef'.**

Around that time you concede defeat and send an email cancelling their service while stuffing fifteen deep-fried Mars Bars down your throat, righteously declaring that diets don't work and you will never achieve the body of your dreams.

Well, you got just one thing right: diets don't work!

The only way you will truly transform your body is to permanently change the way you live your life. That means breaking old habits and replacing them with healthy ones. Sound simple? It is. I promise.

It takes longer to break a habit than it does to create a habit so you have to work on both simultaneously. The good news is it takes only 21 days to create a new habit so keep going.

I remember crying my heart out at week eight, devastated at the thought of never eating pizza again. I was breaking up with my 'best friend' and I couldn't imagine what life would be like without her. By that stage I had a whole range of new healthy habits, all of which were giving me great success on the scales, but the eight-week break-up was devastatingly difficult to survive.

Fast forward a few months, and I was 50 kilos lighter and running the City to Surf fun-run. I discovered there was more to life than eating junk food. It just took a little bit of time and persistence to convince my mind and body to work as one.

I still eat pizza, just not in the quantities I used to, and I rarely follow it with the deep-fried chicken wings, garlic bread and chocolate cheesecake.

Let me reassure you: you are not alone. This is normal. You are not a freak or a failure and it does get easier. You've spent the last ten years snacking on Snickers bars for morning tea.

It may take you two months to break that habit, but once it's gone—no more brightly lit changing-room blues for you baby! This is where you truly transform your body and your life.

**Be prepared.** Face the crash and burn head on and you will overcome it. Know what it is you crave and have healthy substitutes on hand. If chocolate brings you unstuck buy the Atkins Chocolate Indulgence bar (it's bloody brilliant), or Nestlé diet chockie mousse (yum). If hot chips beckon, get the Weight Watcher's frozen healthy version. If you love pizza make your own. I promise you, your thighs (and your heart) will thank you.

**Keep moving.** Exercise gives you that added boost to help you make healthy choices. The endorphin rush is fabulous and if your gym is anything like mine, those spunky half-naked guys pumping weights are an added incentive for not chowing down on fifteen hot dogs for breakfast.

**Remind yourself of your goals.** Get out those skinny jeans. Squeeze into them, even if you have to lie on the floor using a coat hanger to zip them up. Notice how much closer you are to getting them on comfortably, or in my case, how close you are to being able to walk in them without mushrooming out over the top. Listen to hypnosis or motivational CDs. Pin positive mantras around the house. On my fridge I have a sign that says: Stop. Think about it. Do you really want to wear that on your bum? It works…almost every time.

**Reward yourself often.** Don't go without. Living off salad and fresh air will only make you binge on what it is you really crave. Have a little bit of everything, but everything in moderation. Find alternative rewards to food. Buy a new dress or some jewellery, treat yourself to a night out.

**Most importantly of all, persevere.** You deserve the very best in life so do not stop until you have it. Remember: three steps forward and one step back is still two steps forward! And if all else fails: bluff it until you become it. Act like a healthy person until you become a healthy person.

# AFTERNOON GRAZING

**This is one of my toughest areas and I understand how hard it can be to deal with. It is difficult for a few reasons—hunger, habit, boredom, addiction, stress.**

When you step away from the problem and look at it from a different angle, you can sometimes see it in a way that is much easier to understand and therefore overcome.

Let's start with:

1.   Hunger

   ❀   Are you really hungry or do you just want to eat?

   ❀   Have you eaten enough food during the day to sustain your energy levels?

   ❀   Have you had fruit and protein already? Are you skimping on lunch in the hope of speeding your weight loss?

   ❀   Are you having too many carbs, or are they all high GI?

   ❀   Have you had enough to drink?

   ❀   Are you eating at the right times?

   ❀   Are you having protein in the afternoon?

2.   Boredom

   ❀   Is eating food more productive than the million other things you have to do? Make a list of things you will do as soon as you have had your snack. Do them.

   ❀   Keep a journal of why you think you are bored. Name what makes your life so boring, then go out and do some of the stuff that will make it not so boring.

   ❀   If you are bored do something other than eating. It is totally within your capabilities.

3.   Habit

   ❀   The best way to break a habit is to create a new one. It will take you three weeks so start now.

4. Addiction

✿ Do you really think that if you don't eat that chocolate bar or coffee scroll, you will get the shakes and go into spasms because you are addicted to food?

✿ Unless you are diabetic then you can't really need the food that you claim to be 'addicted' to. Go back to keeping a journal. How do you feel? Controlled? How could that be when you are the one who is in control at all times? Depressed? Because you can't have the scroll or because the longing for the scroll replaces what you are really depressed about? Why don't you forget the scroll and write down what it is you are really feeling? If there are things that make you sad, actively spend your 'eating' time on doing what it takes to change that.

5. Stress

✿ There are no studies showing that eating reduces your levels of stress. On the other hand, many studies do show that exercise reduces stress. Spend the 20 minutes you'd have wasted making a grilled cheese sandwich on having a banana and walking around the block picking your neighbours' flowers. Exercise releases endorphins, a natural high better than any drug, and the flowers you pick will make you happy.

Call it what it is: the truth will set you free. Look after yourself; look into yourself; listen to yourself; see what it is you truly desire and go after that. It is so much more satisfying.

# Charity Begins at Home

**I would categorically like to apologise to my son Kai for ruining his entire Kindergarten year by being the one mum who did NOT take part in the Krispy Kreme fundraising drive. I acknowledge that he didn't understand how he could have taken $20 to school just like all the other kids, and not get the box of sticky finger-licking sprinkle-filled joy.**

He could not have known that the piece of paper he took with the money was not an order form, but a lengthy letter shaming the school for using peer group pressure, junk food and sugar addiction to raise money.

He could not have known that the letter explained that I was giving the money to school as a donation for the funds they needed, without them having to give a portion of it to an American company. He wouldn't have read the figures on childhood obesity I quoted. He couldn't have known any of that. He just knew that he was the only kid who took money to school and didn't come home with a box of double-glazed doughnuts.

Most of all, I would like to say that I would do it all again and when I say I am sorry, I should clarify. I am sorry that we are not evolved enough to see that junk food companies who use our children to sell their products in vast quantities are evil. Companies who sell anything unhealthy under the guise that they are helping your school or your charity are evil. Any of us who fall for it should be ashamed of ourselves. That is what I am sorry for.

Next time someone comes around selling chocolates, candy, doughnuts, hamburgers, cookies, telling you it is 'for the children', ask them what they intend to do 'for the children' when the cardiac wards are full and the transplant list too long to service a third of them.

Spend time researching healthy fundraising alternatives that promote awareness, understanding and compassion for the plight of others, rather than selling unhealthy products to children who know no better. And the next time you reach into the charity chocolate box convincing yourself you are doing a good deed, drop the money in without taking anything out. Even better, go directly to the website of the charity, bypass the candy company's profit-making and donate the total amount to the people who need it most.

# Don't Panic, It's Just Hunger

**I don't know about you, but sometimes I panic when I get hungry. At the first twinge of hunger I immediately turn to food. Almost the very second I get the first rumble.**

But what is wrong with hunger? Hunger is the body's way of asking for permission to burn fat, so you should look forward to it. You get hungry because your fuel has run out. Getting hungry indicates your metabolism is working on all cylinders.

But consider this for a moment: is it actually almost time to eat?

Every time you feel hungry, leave it for half an hour or so and give your body permission to burn a little more fat before tucking into a meal.

Honest hunger is that amazing feeling you get after exercise. Knowing that I have used up everything I have eaten and that my body is asking for fuel makes me truly appreciate my next meal.

If you are eating enough of the right kinds of food, you should only be getting genuinely hungry around meal times. Sometimes our brain misinterprets thirst for hunger so have a couple of glasses of water first. Recognise whether you just want to eat instead of being genuinely hungry. If you want to eat something then perhaps you are seeking something else .

If you never feel hunger it is because your metabolism has come to a standstill. In fat-burning mode you will feel hungry. Just remember: hunger is a good thing, you won't die from it so don't panic! Eat regularly, eat well and eat if you are hungry—just make sure you are and don't be afraid to burn a little fat first.

# You ARE What You Eat

**I want you to have a look at how I use a food diary to assess the changes I make in my eating habits week by week. It is a constant process. The whole idea is to put you in control of your healthy body goals.**

I write everything down and have a look at it at the end of the week. Then I recommit to the next week. I write up more mantras and more plans, and I decide to do things a little better. Learn, adapt, grow.

*Food Diary—first week.*

*THURSDAY*
*B: 2 eggs on toast, ½ cup juice*
*S: Chocolate*
*L: Lean Cuisine*
*S: Special K bar*
*D: Protein shake or bar*
*S: Protein bar*
*Exercise: Soccer training 2 hours*

*FRIDAY*
*B: 2 crumpets with Marmite*
*S: ½ protein bar*
*L: Beef and salad on roll*
*S: Peaches on Filo and 2 potato scallops*
*D: Pasta with tomato base, spinach and ricotta*
*S: None*
*Exercise: Bay walk*

SATURDAY
B: 2 crumpets
S: Protein shake
L: 2 eggs on roll
S: Banana and low-fat ice cream
D: Crab pastry plate or chicken breast, roast veggies
S: Taste of lemon dessert, 3 wines, 1 Schnapps
Exercise: Pump, 4km walk.

SUNDAY
B: Baked beans on toast
S: None
L: 100% beef burger and 6 chips
S: Yoghurt
D: 2 minute noodles
S: Egg on toast
Exercise: Soccer 80 mins
Comments: Playing soccer during morning
snack time.

MONDAY
B: Sultana Bran, cup of milk
S: Popcorn
L: Smoked salmon and cream cheese bagel
S: Protein bar
D: Lean cuisine, peanut butter on wholegrain bread
S: Yoghurt
Exercise: Pump (1 hour)

## TUESDAY

B: 2 crumpets
S: Small Easter egg
L: ½ low-fat cheese and tomato toasted sandwich
S: Special K bar
D: Lean Cuisine
S: None
Exercise: Day off

## WEDNESDAY

B: 2 crumpets/yoghurt
S: Protein shake
L: 2 eggs on Multigrain
S: Banana
D: Lean Cuisine
S: None
Exercise: Weights session.

## AJAY'S FOOD DIARY BREAKDOWN

(extract from Food Diary April 2004: returning to healthy eating post back injury)

Thursday: Had a late breakfast (thus no snack) as I slept in. This is okay but only occasionally. Should have had more fruit. I train through dinner so take a protein shake and bar with me so I eat as soon as I finish.

Friday: Not eating enough food, or even enough fruit. Will definitely increase my food intake next week, particularly at breakfast time. Will try to add a piece of fruit or yoghurt every morning. Had a breakout with the scallops! Went shopping without my own snack and therefore crashed and burned. Lesson for the day: always be prepared.

*Saturday: Ate well on my birthday. Made sure I did a workout and a walk knowing I would eat and drink more tonight. Literally dragged my old self out of bed but felt better having done it. Loved the endorphin rush after. Made good choices at birthday dinner—ate very small portion of crab for entrée, ordered chicken breast for main and opted for a small taste of my partner's lemon dessert. Once again reminded myself of the bigger picture and congratulated myself on making good choices that I will benefit from next birthday! Drank moderately. Good girl!*

*Sunday: was playing soccer so I ate a protein breakfast that would sustain me as I would be playing through my snack time. Ate a rather big burger for lunch with an egg (YUM) and bacon (oops!)—heavy on the protein after such a big workout—over 90 minutes! Did sneak a few chips as I forgot to order the meal without them. Control what you get on your plate. Ate lightly at dinner to compensate.*

*Monday: ate well this day, starting to get into the right habits, waking up very hungry. Still need to eat more fruit and more food generally. It's school holidays and I am rushed off my feet. Went to cinema straight after pump class, forgot wallet and forgot to take protein bar or shake—therefore ate my son's popcorn at the movies (very bad). Need to make myself and my food choices a priority and need to get into the habit of being prepared. I know this but it will take me a few weeks and perhaps a few lost kilos (or not lost kilos) to remind myself of the importance of this.*

*Tuesday is my exercise-free day. Allows my body to recover from soccer and weights. I make sure I eat lightly on these days but the Easter egg didn't help. Got rid of all eggs and chocolate from house. I asked myself what I was missing out on. The eggs? Or being able to fit into my skinny jeans? The jeans won out and the carers at vacation care got a bag full of eggs and a box of Lindt chocolate balls. Ajay is a legend. Told myself that often.*

*Wednesday: Same as most days, good choices, but need to eat more fruit.*

*Goal for next week is to eat more fruit, more at breakfast and to always be prepared. Am going light on alcohol just to give my body that extra little boost in getting started. This was a great first week (compared with the pizza, Oporto, Nandos and champagne of last week) and would hope to rely less on Lean Cuisines as time goes by but are a great support in the meantime. Need to substitute fruit for Special K bars but again it's about taking baby steps.*

*Exercise levels were good. Got my one extra walk in this week (in fact, looking back I realise I did two! Woohoo!) did three weights sessions, trained soccer (two hours) and played soccer (90 mins) which is most definitely my cardio quotient for the week.*

*Exercise goal this week is to add three walks and some stair work.*

*Can't wait to monthly measure! I am changing my body.*

I forgive myself my mistakes and refine my whole approach to eating. Simply deciding to improve snack choices will make next week more successful.

**Tips for having a better food diary your first few weeks**

- ❀ Eat breakfast. Eat it early. The sooner you eat breakfast the sooner your metabolism gets fired up.
- ❀ Eat more at breakfast. A muesli bar is not a staple breakfast. Porridge and fruit, cereal and fruit, muesli and fruit, toast and yogurt and a piece of fruit are all okay.
- ❀ Make sure you don't miss your snacks (I mean it!).
- ❀ Don't eat a main meal at a snack time.
- ❀ Full strength Coca cola or any soda is not good. One a day is too much.
- ❀ Drink more water.
- ❀ Stay away from cordial.
- ❀ Watch out for coffee. It dehydrates you.
- ❀ If you insist on eating chocolate then have it before midday. You'll burn it off.
- ❀ Eat low-fat versions of everything—ham, cheese, milk, butter, cream, etc.
- ❀ Biscuits are not the best option for snacks. Have fruit and one biscuit rather than just three or four biscuits. You will fill yourself up more and have something that is better for you.

- ❀ Curries are out for the time being. So is pad Thai and peanut sauce. If you're feeling ambitious get online, find low-fat versions and make them yourself, but remember portion control will help you just as much as using low-fat substitutes.
- ❀ Start cutting down the lollies.
- ❀ Do not buy Tim Tams or anything else like that. If you really want a Tim Tam, buy the little ones from the servo. That way you keep the temptation out of your house.
- ❀ Cut down on alcohol.

I have said it a million times but I will say it again. Truth is power. The more you connect with what you are actually doing instead of what you convince yourself you are doing, the sooner you will reach your goals. I can't tell you how often someone will say to me, 'but I eat healthily', and then they record what they eat and it's enough for three breastfeeding women.

Now pick up the pen and get writing: it is your new sword for fighting the fat demon and you are going to win this battle.

# 'Eat, Drink and Be Merry, For Tomorrow We Diet'

**I know you are ALL going on a diet first thing Monday morning. I'm sure you were inspired by the cover of some magazine that had Kelly Osborne or Kim Kardashian's latest crazy regime and this time, this time for sure, you know this one will work for you. You did the grapefruit, lemon juice, cabbage leaf, tomato soup, apples only diets and failed at every one of them, but this one just seems so much more possible.**

Let me tell you something before you go throwing out your bread bins or fruit baskets: crazy crash dieting does not work.

I was hosting *The Biggest Loser* and the crazy 20-hour days and catering on set had me struggling to maintain my weight. Just when I was feeling vulnerable, which happens when random strangers write to you and tell you to get your own butt on a treadmill,  everyone I knew suggested I do 'the protein thing' to really cut down quickly.

Everyone was trying to convince me it was a good thing to do—to sacrifice living a healthy, normal-bodied life just to squeeze down an extra few kilos. When did God make the handbook that states all television hosts should be a size 6?

A few days after foolishly reading some nasty fat-bashing blogs about myself, my editor at *Cleo* magazine asked if I would write about the negative effects of cutting out whole food groups in an attempt to lose weight.

I put myself and a friend onto the protein diet, becoming the ultimate crash diet dummies. I would be the human guinea pig and see what the hoo-ha was all about. After about day six I had no idea why anyone in their right mind would do it, no matter how much weight they lost.

We basically lived off meat and the odd 'allowed' veggie. Alcohol was gone; sugar was gone; chocolate; bread—everything except meat, meat and more meat. I was eating a million eggs, nuts, high-fat protein bars and if I'd done it 'properly' I could have had sausages and bacon and chicken with the skin on. But while my waistline was shrinking due to the body going into what is called ketosis (basically it is so hungry for carbs it strips the fat), I couldn't help but think of my poor heart and the hardened arteries I would end up with.

My mouth smelled and tasted like sweaty socks that were never washed. Even my personal trainer complained of my fetid breath. I didn't go to the toilet for days as no carbs means no fruit or cereal, meaning no fibre. Ouch! By day five I was farting like a baked-bean-eating champion and was so tired I could barely get out of bed let alone actually do any decent form of exercise. I was starving, craving everything, and day six saw me wanting to chew food and spit it out just for the taste.

I missed the sugar in my tea. I missed having cereal for breakfast. I wanted a piece of fruit or some yoghurt or, God forbid, a bread roll with dinner. I couldn't eat out with my friends, toast my friends at their wedding or taste my son's birthday cake. If that wasn't bad enough, every time I stood up my head spun. I had a headache and I was miserable and I quit faster than you can say 'two-all beef patties, no sauce, special cheese, pickles, onion not on a sesame seed bun.'

I lost 1.4 kilos in a week and my friend (who lived off diet cola, protein shakes and Reductil) lost 3 kilos in a week, but she was miserable too.

Unless you go off it slowly, the weight will come crashing back on again. Your metabolism is shot to pieces and you are likely to go on a backlash binge of anything even remotely resembling a carb. My friend crashed spectacularly, finishing off a large pizza, garlic bread, huge packet of M&Ms and seventeen beers.

The stupid thing is we can all lose a kilo in a week, while still having a wine after dinner, eating bread, fruit and grains, and having a life. What's the point of suffering so much just to lose weight a little bit faster? I would rather get a little grief over my bigger-than-average TV host body than give up whole food groups just to look a certain way by 5pm Friday. Whatever the 'diet' is, it will never be as good as living and eating healthily. Any 'diet' high in fat is dangerous in the long term. Any 'diet' cutting out any food group is unhealthy, restrictive and unsustainable. Who wants to make scurvy fashionable again? It is no accident the man who invented the Atkins diet died obese.

If you eat healthy portions of all the food groups, exercise often, and don't drink to excess, you will be healthy and have a body that reflects that. Everything else is stupid, short-term, unhealthy and not worth suffering for. For goodness sake, do as your mother said and eat your greens!

# Busy Hands

**Why is it that when we go to the football or movies, or even just sit in front of the TV, we feel the need to graze on food we just don't need? A lot of people call it comfort eating, something they've simply become 'comfortable' doing. I just call it a bad habit. There is nothing comfortable about trying to squeeze your body into a bikini one week out of summer in a brightly lit change room with no lock on it.**

Instead of diving into the popcorn, knit or crochet little five by five squares instead. Make a little basket full of different colours and textures of wool, a little like a yummy mixed lolly bag. Every time you are idle and prone to eat like a robot, knit one, pearl one to your heart's delight.

When you have enough little squares, sew them all together. You now have a beautiful warm homemade blanket you can either give to your kids or donate to the needy. Or send them to me, and my healthy body club army of girls will collect them, sew them together and send them out.

Best of all, you won't end up with your own personal blanket of fat you have to work twice as hard to get rid of.

# ADDICTIVE BEHAVIOUR

**A drug addict who injects himself with heroin does not call it 'comfort smack', even though he feels good when he takes it.**

And the addicts who know the drugs are killing them don't justify them with, 'they make me feel better, they really do.' Those trying to get off the drugs acknowledge the addiction, and accept that while they feel good temporarily the drugs are doing long-term harm.

So why be so stubborn with 'addictive' behaviours such as bingeing, eating crap food and not exercising? Why lie to yourself? Why not deal with it as an addiction, rather than continue to tell yourself it is something else? Of course, you are not actually addicted to bad food but it's a useful way to treat the problem.

If I drink too much I do not call it comfort drinking. I call it drinking too much. I choose to feel good temporarily while seriously sabotaging my goals.

Call it what it is and see how long you continue to do it. As you binge say to yourself, 'I am choosing to do something that does nothing for my long-term health, nothing for my goals and will only serve to keep me from being where I actually want to be. This will not make me any happier tomorrow.'

Everything has a cost. Be honest when you weigh up the choices and you may find the choices become easier.

# HONEY ARE WE KILLING THE KIDS?

**In the last few years we have heard scary statistics about the 'obesity epidemic', particularly in relation to our children. One in four of our kids is obese. Another one of those four is overweight and on the way to obesity. A great many parents with overweight children don't even know it.**

Is it because everyone has got so chubby we don't even know what's normal and healthy any more? Are we guilty of only seeing our kids through rose-coloured glasses? Do we explain it away with 'he's eating for three because he's about to have a growth spurt'? Whatever the answer is, it is about time we, as parents, accept responsibility for the way our children are.

If your child is significantly overweight they have a huge chance of getting type 2 diabetes by the time they become a teenager. I know you really don't think about what you are doing when you cave in to their every demand, but let me put it you this way: if I handed you a syringe marked 50milligrams of obesity, would you inject your child with it?

One meal from a fast food 'restaurant' can equal, and sometimes double, your child's recommended daily allowance of fat and calories. My son is lucky if he goes through the drive-through once every three months. He doesn't bother asking me any more, and sometimes when I suggest it he is the one who says no.

Even if your kid eats 'reasonably well' throughout the week, it all adds up. If you counted the incidental foods like chips, lollies, soft drink, cordial, ice blocks, doughnuts, biscuits and bubble gum, you may be surprised at the result. The food you give your child has a very real impact on them—not only now but on the person they become later in life. Teach them to appreciate all different kinds of foods, broaden their tastes and educate them on making healthy choices.

A lot of you will say 'my kid's a fussy eater'. You have the ability to change that. If your child is hungry they will eat. And even better, the more new foods you give them the more they will like—eventually.

You don't have to totally substitute chicken nuggets with a full plate of broccoli tonight.

But put one piece of broccoli down, and when they eat that they can have the nuggets. Start out slowly. Don't force them, but do reward them for trying new things. I've been hiding mushrooms, capsicum, broccoli, zucchini, tomato and carrot in spaghetti bolognaise for years. Now my son will try almost anything once, happily eats fresh steamed veggies and when we eat out he often opts for some exotic pasta.

I made the rules and I enforced them. I endured the tantrums when he wanted hot chips. He does get hot chips, just not every time we leave the house. He may prefer chocolate-coated muesli bars for a snack, but if I only have grapes, strawberries and apples with me then he doesn't have a choice. In the worst-case scenario, he can have the muesli bar after eating the fruit but chances are he will be too full to have anything else.

I hate to say this, but I truly believe making your kids obese is bordering on child abuse. Don't tell me it is cheaper to eat takeaway. I know what it costs to feed a family if you go into the drive-through, and for the same amount of money you can make a huge pot of delicious soup that will last two or even three meals.

It's your job as a parent to teach them how to be, so give it your best shot. You might be surprised how successful you can be.

# WINTER BLUES

**Ah, winter. Open fires, toasted marshmallows, hot chocolate, more toasted marshmallows, red wine and chocolates in bed with the electric blanket on high. Then there's pea and ham soup, roast dinners with lots of baked veggies and lashings of gravy, and rainy days where you just stay in, rugging up in tracky daks with elasticised waists and oversized jumpers.**

Three months later, you realise with horror that the only way you are going to fit into your jeans is if you chainsaw your bum in half, using a crowbar to squeeze the rest of the flesh in and a tow truck to winch up the zip.

So how do we avoid that dreaded—and seemingly inevitable—winter weight gain? It's easy, just eat lettuce, work out in the rain every day, catch pneumonia and you will instantaneously lose bucketloads of weight.

Not very inspiring is it? Nor does it sound like much fun. Give yourself a break. Stop stressing about it, put a few simple strategies in place and you may find that not only do you not gain weight in winter, you may be one of the few who actually lose weight for summer.

Planning and preparation make all the difference. Know where you come unstuck and tackle those issues head on.

First step: exercise. If you normally run but don't want to when it is cold and rainy, hire a treadmill or join a gym for three months just to get you through. If you can't get motivated at 6am when it's dark and so cold your breakfast Mars bar freezes, arrange to meet a friend or book a personal training session. You are less likely to back out if someone is expecting you.

Join a team sport that runs through winter. Try football, rugby, hockey, indoor soccer or netball. Don't worry if you've never played before: most sporting associations have beginner divisions with a coach who will teach you how to play. Despite having two left feet, I started soccer at the age of 31 and almost never manage to embarrass myself completely. If I can do it anyone can.

And instead of hiding under all the extra layers, think of it as keeping a great secret. Cover up your body transformation and surprise your friends in summer.

Inspire yourself. Buy a dress or some jeans a little too tight and make it your goal to fit into them by the end of winter. Try them on once a month and reward yourself (not with food—have a pedicure instead) every time that zip gets a little closer to going all the way up.

Buy low-fat recipe books. You'll be surprised how much yummy 'comfort' food you can cook. Have warm salads with protein and soups are great—just make them healthy and low-fat. Instead of big blocks of chocolate try mini Turkish delights. Everything is okay—in moderation.

When you are sitting in front of the TV, nurture yourself. You'll be amazed how great your nails and feet look after three months of pampering. Keep your hands busy and you won't overeat.

Treat yourself well and find yourself healthier, fitter and feeling better in just three months' time. And if something goes wrong, forgive yourself and start again. Remember, it's not a race. You have the rest of your life to enjoy the benefits of good health so just keep going.

# Bingeing: the Truth

According to my dictionary, a binge is a period of excessive and unrestrained self-indulgence in food or drink.

The key words here are 'excessive' and 'unrestrained'.

There are no benefits to be gained from bingeing. I remember eating as much as I wanted of what I wanted, meal after meal. It never stopped and makes me sick to think about now.

I had many different ways of bingeing—some were planned feasts and others meant eating a surplus of whatever I wanted, whenever I wanted it.

Why? Because I had nothing of substance going on in my life. That is the truth.

Healthy people do not binge. They have moments of indulgence but they do not binge. There is a huge difference.

Either you are bingeing or you are not. Either you want to stop or you don't. If you really want to stop, and you can't, seek professional help. I did and I don't remember the last time I had a binge.

The freedom I feel from not having that horrible post-binge self-hatred is almost impossible to describe. Enjoying indulgent food occasionally tastes much better than any food eaten during a binge.

This may sound harsh but I am desperately trying to reach those who have given up—those who have convinced themselves it is okay. It's not and if you want to live a healthy life you only have two options:

1. Stop bingeing or,
2. Get help to stop bingeing.

There is NO option where it will EVER be okay.

Make rules; have plans; keep trying until you succeed. There are hundreds of things you can do instead of eating crappy food that does nothing for your body or your quality of life.

The key is to keep trying until you find what works for you, but make a commitment right here, right now to never stop trying until you have successfully given up bingeing forever.

Trust me, life as a healthy person tastes so much sweeter.

# CHOICES

**This started out being called 'Sacrifices'. It was going to be a list of habits I had 'given up' to lose weight and stay that way. As I thought it through, I realised I had actually given up very little: I had merely made changes.**

I gave up cheese…but I didn't really. I don't eat anything with cheese in a restaurant, but I still eat lite cheese at home.

I gave up junk food…except I still eat chips, hot dogs, hamburgers and pizza. I just get healthy versions in the supermarket or make them myself.

I gave up beer… even though you can now get low-carb beer, I did give this one the toss. It is extra calories I don't need.

I gave up lollies… I slowly weaned myself off them. These days I have jelly lollies only occasionally.

I gave up dessert…I have tiny slices when I want, but these days I generally say, 'I don't do dessert'. And I believe it.

The list could go on forever.

Next time you contemplate your choices, realise they are not sacrifices. Gaining a healthy body is not going without. It is what you choose to eat, do, think and be that will make you the way you are: so choose a healthy body!

# Friday Night Smackdown

**Monday is early morning Pilates followed by wheatgrass shots and alfalfa sprouts for breakfast. Tuesday is cardio funk, four bottles of water, brown rice and veggies finished off with a shiatsu massage. Wednesday is a hardcore spin class and nothing that doesn't grow on trees for food. Thursday is sunrise yoga and a sunset 5 kilometre run along the beach. Friday sees you do a lunchtime cardio class followed by a healthy salad sitting at your desk while sipping your fourth water and your second green tea of the day. Damn you're good!**

Then the wildebeest takes over, and some time in the wee hours of Saturday morning you are seen tabletop dancing, before stumbling out the door on your way to the greasy kebab or pizza shop. The morning hangover calls for a fry-up, followed by hair of the dog, and once again you are last seen falling in a taxi that has been convinced to go via the drive-through.

Sunday, after waking with half a burger in your hand, has you spending the first half of the day nursing your wounds, eating chocolate and finishing with a long lunch with friends—maybe even a Sunday roast with enough baked veggies to feed a third world country. Meanwhile, the closest you came to cross-training was having a beer in one hand and a pie in the other.

If you eat well and exercise during the week then that's half the battle. At least you know what to do. But do the maths. Four weekends a month is more than an entire week put together. Imagine if you ate like that every day for eight days straight.

I'm not being the fun police. What's the point of working hard all week to not kick back in your time off? You just need to tweak it a little. Set up some simple rules to help you through.

Try meeting with friends for an early morning hike or a walk along the beach instead of the long Sunday lunch. Prepare an indulgent fruit salad or your own Bircher muesli on a Friday night so you know what you are having Saturday morning. You won't have to even think about the greasy heart attack fry-up. Eight-course degustation dinners can be turned into healthy home-cooked dinner parties for friends.

Simple changes can make a world of difference. You don't have to stay at home alone just because you want to live more healthily. Just incorporate it into your life.

Consider making a deal with yourself that every second week you'll curb the Friday night drinking, and instead get up early and meet a girlfriend for a Saturday morning spin class, followed by a relaxing massage or facial

You might even relax a little more through the week with an occasional glass of wine so you don't swing in the complete opposite direction on weekends. By taking the pressure off yourself you may not feel the need to cut so loose.

Find a balance you can manage and the weekends can be your friend again.

# FOOD CUES

**You have trained yourself to eat certain foods so well, you actually believe you don't like healthy food. I believed I didn't like anything healthy. I used to think I was missing out if I didn't order the fattiest meal on the menu. When I first started making changes, I really didn't enjoy the meals. Fruit was boring and tasteless and vegetables were a nightmare.**

Slowly, that started to change. The more fruit I ate the more I craved. The more I experimented with what was on the menu, the more foods I discovered were delicious and healthy.

The next step was to avoid situations that helped me sabotage my goals.

I used to enter my local shopping centre through the food hall. I now go in the long way and walk up the stairs so I avoid the donut shop, the fish and chip shop and the Chinese all-you-can-eat buffet. I don't believe in willpower: you just have to create a safe environment. Out of sight can eventually become out of mind.

Staying healthy takes dedication, patience, understanding, education and honesty. You have to scrutinise your life and investigate where the triggers are.

Some examples are:

- ❀ The drive-through—driving past it, seeing it, fantasising about it.
- ❀ Aroma of food—the smell of cooking while out walking, chocolate shops.
- ❀ Vending machines—on the train station, at work.
- ❀ Your office—kitchen, where it is situated, what you have to walk past to get there, what other people eat.
- ❀ Your car—what's in the console, listening to the ads on the radio, passing regular food joints.
- ❀ The movies—we all know about that one.
- ❀ TV—icecream in bed, lollies, biscuits.
- ❀ In bed.
- ❀ The way you go to work.

- ❀ Parties.
- ❀ Vacations.
- ❀ Ads on TV.
- ❀ Reading.
- ❀ Sight of food.
- ❀ Being offered food.
- ❀ Time (watching the clock).
- ❀ Flavour—salty, sweet, etc. can be highly addictive.

As soon as you start to think about these foods, you salivate—that can make you think you are hungry. Then the emotional link kicks in and you convince yourself you need that particular food to make you happy, otherwise you feel you are missing out.

Here are some ways to approach each situation:

- ❀ The drive-through—don't drive past it, keep fruit in the console of the car.
- ❀ Aroma of food—wear perfume and every time you focus on the smell of the food sniff your wrist. Drink water every time you salivate.
- ❀ Vending machines—stand away from them. Ring the supplier and ask to put healthier choices in them. Plan to carry snacks yourself.
- ❀ Your office—leave the office at lunchtime and sit in the park. Never walk into or out of the office starving. Take your own lunch. Never plan meetings over lunch.
- ❀ Your car—ban all food from it. It will be cleaner and you will be healthier for it.
- ❀ The movies—have a protein shake before leaving home. Take your own microwave low-fat popcorn. Knit to keep your hands busy.
- ❀ TV—do your nails, have a hot chocolate.
- ❀ In bed—the only food you should ever have in bed is chocolate body paint and I'm pretty sure that does not come in a low-fat version.
- ❀ The way you go to work—avoid. Find a new way.
- ❀ Parties—take your own plate, arrive late, stand well away from the table, have water on hand at all times.

- ❀ Vacations—have rules written out and paste them on your hotel fridge. Do a shop as soon as you arrive or take healthy snacks with you. Plan your week. Go for a run every morning on waking or a walk at sunset—no excuses.
- ❀ Ads on TV—do sit-ups, leave the room, read a book, knit.
- ❀ Reading—have a foot spa, hand spa or manicure (you can't eat while your nails are drying).
- ❀ Sight of food—don't look at it, walk away. If you are standing next to food you can't stop eating then stand somewhere else, dummy!
- ❀ Being offered food—say you are allergic, say you've already eaten, say you'll have some later, just say NO!
- ❀ Time (watching the clock)—ask yourself if you are hungry. Find out how long it has been since you last ate. If you are training your metabolism you must eat every three or so hours. If you have already done so and it is not time to eat then drink water instead.
- ❀ Flavour—find that 'flavour' in a healthy option (if you are craving sweets, have a fruit salad or diet jelly).

Ask yourself what you are really missing out on by staying the way you are. That food will always be around in abundance. You can have it later, or as a healthy version. You may never actually crave it again.

It's in your hands—whether they are holding a burger and fries or are driving you to the gym. Your choice. Your life. You know what to do.

# Fit and Fabulous

'It is hard to fail, but it is worse never to have tried to succeed.'

*Theodore Roosevelt*

# Beat the Clock

**You joined the gym, bought new runners and paid a fortune for designer workout gear. You even had your eyelashes tinted so that sweating makes you look HOT and NOT like you are entering an Alice Cooper look-alike competition.**

But every day since you joined that 6am spin class, you have set the alarm clock for 5.30am and, after a quick swipe of the snooze button, have woken at 8am cursing yourself.

Here's how to do it differently:

First of all, get to bed earlier. Even if you are not tired the first night you will be after three early morning workouts. Try drinking a herbal tea that helps you sleep.

Drink lots of water the day and night before. Hydration is the key to feeling fresh upon waking.

Grab your alarm clock and take it out to the kitchen or living room. Turn it up LOUD! Set your gym gear out next to it—socks on the shoes, everything placed in order so you can throw it on while half asleep. Put your keys, purse, gym card and bag (packed with morning snacks like nuts, fruit or muesli bars) next to that, along with a bottle of water. In winter put a little fan heater next to everything so you can keep warm while you dress.

The next morning, you'll have to get out of bed and into the next room to turn the alarm off. Since you have come this far you may as well just get dressed, get out the door and get your soon-to-be-hot butt into the gym. Easy!

# INCREDIBLE HUNK TRAINING PROGRAM

**I have trouble running a bath, let alone actually running any kind of distance. And yet I have competed in more than a dozen triathlons and decided to run a half and then full marathon. Why? So I am constantly challenging myself to step up and evolve. The more I do that the less likely I will ever return to my old ways.**

The best way to teach yourself to run is with the Incredible Hunk training program. The point is to make running about more than just 'why', 'how far', or 'how many calories you burn'. That's just boring, and way too hard for someone who prefers chocolates that come without wrappers because it is too much effort to unwrap them.

Pick a place that is a popular running spot. There are plenty around: the boardwalk of your local beach, a council-built running track or any public park. Now walk. Yes—just start walking.

When you spot a hunk up ahead of you RUN! I am completely serious. Run up to and past him (you are allowed to sneak a peek at the tush as you pass), then resume walking and catch your breath.

If the hunk happens to be running too, chances are he will pass you again. When you have recovered, run to your original hunk or pick another—as long as they are in front you just have to move quickly until you pass your landmark (or, should I say, your 'man'mark).

The key is to have fun with your fitness regime instead of worrying whether you are doing it right. You can pick any objects to aim for—park benches, trees or lamps—but I find hunks so much more motivating.

Eventually you will be able to run the whole distance, because you will be fitter than you ever knew you could be. Before you know it someone else will be doing the Incredible Hunk training plan on you!

# In a Meeting

**If you went through my diary I would seem to be a very busy woman. I have meetings at either 8.30am or 9am Monday through Friday. On Wednesdays I have an extra special meeting at 10am, and on Saturdays I have a recurring appointment with RC at 8am. These times are blocked out up to a month ahead, and when people ask my availability I work around my appointments unless absolutely necessary.**

The truth is, these 'meetings' are the classes or exercise sessions I have committed to for the next few weeks. By putting them in my diary first I can organise the rest of my month around them, rather than squeezing exercise into whatever time is left over at the end of the day.

'RC' is hiking Runyon Canyon in Los Angeles, my favourite thing to do on a Saturday morning. If friends want to meet up for breakfast they either have to walk with me first or wait for brunch. There will always be people who want priority in your life and try to make you meet their needs before anything else. If you keep drumming your regular times of unavailability into them, they will eventually work around those 'meetings' you just can't miss.

Prioritise your health and the rest of your life will run much more smoothly.

# BURN BABY BURN

**Want to have fun and burn fat at the same time? A hot and steamy sex session can burn around 170 calories an hour (and you don't even have to leave home!)**

A passionate kiss can burn two calories a minute. Ten minutes of kissing can burn 20 calories—and for those scoffing at the not so grand total, it all adds up. A Hershey's Kiss contains 26 calories—thirteen minutes of kissing. I know which one I'd prefer, and no it's not the chocolate.

And for the record, chocolate body paint cancels out the calories burnt but can be fun nonetheless!

# Do Something Different

**They say the definition of madness is doing the same thing over and over and expecting a different outcome. Have you seen girls at the gym using the same exercise bike at the same time each day, going the same speed, reading the latest magazine?**

If you are not shifting weight it may be because your body is not being challenged any more. It's time to change the way you train. Go to the gym at a different time, try a new class, run with someone faster, box with someone fitter, and use different equipment. Swap running for walking or walking for running. Give up the treadmill and take the dog for a walk.

If you've been eating the same foods then change that too. Get up an hour early, have breakfast and go for a walk. Shake it up, surprise yourself and trick your body into kickstarting your metabolism again.

Keep your body guessing to keep complacency at bay.

# Stairway to Heaven

**A friend of mine always takes the stairs. She could be in 10-inch heels and running 15 minutes late but she will side-step the escalator every single time. Let me tell you, this woman is the other side of 50 and not the athletic type.**

When I asked her about it, she said that she had spent quite a bit of time with people who were disabled and didn't have the luxury of using their legs whenever they wanted. To show gratitude for her own physical freedom, she always takes the stairs and uses that time to say a prayer for those not as lucky as some.

Take the stairs whenever you can: you will not only get incidental exercise, but also appreciate the blessings you have. A moment of gratitude can lift the heart instantly.

Now you are ready to take stairs to a whole new level. Scout your local area for a set of stairs; there may only be a few, but if you have a set that the local athletes tackle, then these are your new best friends. Make a date at least once a week to tackle them: fast, slow, up and down, ten times or a hundred. Not only are they great for your legs and butt, they are guaranteed to get your heart pumping and burning calories. If you want to break it up, set yourself some squats, sit-ups or push-ups at the top or the bottom.

If you are just starting out on your journey, do what I did: two steps at a time in my very own house. Yes you heard me: two steps at a time. In my early days of weight loss, I made a commitment to take the first two steps up and down, ten times on each leg, every time I went upstairs. As I got fitter, I added both the top and bottom stairs, and eventually worked my way up to running up and down the whole set ten times in the morning and ten times at night.

Who says you need an expensive gym membership? Stairs are everywhere and you can master them to master your body.

# WALK DON'T RUN!

**One of the best things you can do for weight loss and the planet is walk! Walking is brilliant for burning fat. Would you rather spend thousands of dollars on crazy equipment designed to blitz, lift and blast your body to perfection in x amount of weeks, knowing full well it is just another dust-collecting clothes dryer you are buying?**

Walk everywhere. Walk to the shops; walk to work; walk your kids to school; walk up the stairs; walk down the stairs; walk the dog; walk in the morning; and walk with the kids after dinner. Walk with your friends; walk in a group; walk instead of eating out; walk and talk; walk the walk; and well, just walk! Get the picture?

Save money, save the planet and save yourself.

# 'Reasons' You Can't Exercise

**This really should be called 'Bullshit I tell myself to feel good about being lazy'.**

Let's be honest: there are no reasons for not being able to exercise. They are just excuses and excuses are like arseholes, everyone has one. The only reason you use them is to make yourself feel good about the fact that you are choosing to not achieve your goals. It's that simple.

When we have wheelchair athletes achieving success that able-bodied athletes only dream of, we really have very few justifiable 'reasons' for not doing something.

Just the other day a lady told me (as she walked back and forth to the buffet table at a party) she couldn't exercise cause she had a car accident three years ago.

She nearly choked on her chocolate cake when I called her a liar. I, perhaps not as gently as I could have, explained to her that if she could get up seven times to walk across the room and eat food she does not need, then she could get up once a day and walk around the block.

If you are injured or recovering from an accident, surgery or illness, then do whatever you can. When I broke my leg the first week into my 'diet', I spent months doing exercises in my wheelchair and bed. Then, when able, I got into the pool and swam laps with a waterproof cast on my leg, and I did aquarobics until I was able to walk. Using a cane, I walked as far as I could go and built up my strength from there. One year after my accident, having been told I would never run, I completed a 14 kilometre fun run and came 30,341st out of 60,000 people.

Sure, you can't run a marathon your first day, but if you can walk to the dinner table then you can walk up the street. If you can walk up the street then you can get around the block. If you can get around the block…then you can get what I mean!

# FISHING

**Can't afford a personal trainer but not motivated to run yourself through a series of exercises in the park or the gym? Go fishing.**

I don't mean grabbing a pole and some worms, and sitting by a river. Go to any local big local park or beach on a weekend and you will see all sorts of exercise groups going through the motions. Find one you like and do what they do.

My son has baseball practice every Sunday in a huge park. Just near there is a little group of women who get together and work out. I stand about 50 metres away and simply do whatever it is they do, more or less. If they do push-ups then so do I. When they do step-ups on the park benches I do sprints until they finish, then go and do mine.

There is no end to muscle junkies in the gym who will happily show you how and why they do a particular exercise, especially when you tell them how big their muscles are and ask to feel their huge biceps. Personal trainers are always on the lookout for clients and will often give you a session for free.

Times are tough. Go fish instead.

# OBSERVE AND REPORT

**Having trouble feeling really excited about exercising? You are not alone. The reason we revere athletes so much is their undying dedication to becoming the best they can be. These people are worthy of our admiration.**

I absolutely understand and acknowledge your complete lack of desire to train seven hours a day, seven days a week for 17 years, living off a scientifically controlled diet, all in the slim hope of taking home a gold medal. But what can you do to get yourself up off that couch and to the gym, out for a run, or even taking the kids to the park?

As you go about the rest of your week, take note of the type of people you see exercising.

When you see that hot guy running with his shirt off chase him… no, don't do that, but take the time to admire how his hard work has paid off. Say to yourself, 'he looks like that because he makes the time to go for a run'.

When you pass that bouncy blonde in the Juicy Couture pants walking the dog at 6am when you are just coming home from a few 'after-work drinks', repress the urge to call her nasty names and instead say to yourself, 'she looks great because she sets her alarm to wake up and makes the effort to get her metabolism firing'.

When you walk by the gym, notice how fit, healthy, happy and energised the majority of these people look. Remind yourself that they look like that because they do something about it.

There's no point saying, 'I don't go to the gym because there are only hot skinny people there.' That's just dumb. It's like saying you don't want to get paid cause only rich people have money. The sooner you invest in yourself the sooner it will pay off. The sooner you get to the gym the sooner you will look like them.

# MUSIC SPEAKS TO YOU

**Studies have shown that your heart rate can increase with the beat of the music you listen to. There is no doubt that the Kenny Loggins' Footloose soundtrack gets me up on the dance floor every single time.**

Increasing your heart rate enables you to burn more calories. How good does that sound? Just listen to fast music and lose all the weight you want without ever dieting or even getting up off the couch. Oh, I wish!

Seriously though, listening to music with a faster beat increases your heart rate, so it stands to reason that if you do it while exercising you will burn even more calories. Try running around the park to a slow depressing ballad about losing your man, your dog and your tractor and you are more likely to run into the local bar and drown your sorrows.

Music can make us happy or sad, energised or relaxed. Use music to motivate you. Fill your iPod with fast-paced, go get 'em songs that will inspire you to run faster, jump higher, work harder. Pick music that lifts your spirit and makes you glad you kicked your ex to the curb. The next time you see him, you can laugh over that sexy, finely sculpted shoulder as you walk away humming your favourite tune.

# TRY SOMETHING NEW

**Remember me? I was that slightly chubby kid at school who was always picked last for teams. Kids would pick crippled ants over having me on their side, groaning when it came down to me or the kid with really smelly feet.**

Running races were humiliation parades as even the kids in the next heat beat me over the line. It's no wonder that in high school, sports carnivals were always handled with an 'Ajay had a head cold' note forged after I had spent the day hanging around my local milk bar playing Pacman and eating fish and chips.

Sadly I was never blessed with any kind of natural athletic ability. My brother was the standout sports star and I was…well, at best, the writer (best described as the nerdy schoolie type). I'll never forget my brother being picked for the state boys cricket and soccer teams, and my grandmother handing him ten dollars and telling him how much the ladies like professional sportsmen. She then turned to me and said that I would have to rely on my brains and work ethic to get ahead in life, because I had neither talent nor looks.

I avoided all school sports by editing the school newspaper and yearbook. Every PE lesson involving team sport saw me having 'that time of the month' every day of the week for months on end, until they eventually gave up and handed me the mascot outfit. Even that didn't fit!

Ten years later I made a conscious decision to become a very different person to the one who had piled on the kilos. I decided I was never going to say, 'I'm not sporty' again. I was new and improved, and fitness, sport, and the gym were my as-yet-undiscovered friends.

First I became a gym junkie. I actually found myself craving pump classes on a Saturday morning instead of nursing a hangover. I found that if I missed the gym for any length of time I became depressed and not 'myself'.

Then I became a runner. Well, I ran; calling myself a runner is a bit like Paris Hilton calling herself a lady. I started out doing small fun runs for charity, and despite it never being easy I revelled in the challenge.

My biggest challenge was making sure my boobs didn't give me black eyes. Then I just wanted to finish the distance. Next I wanted to run the whole race, then, being slightly addictive in nature, I wanted to go from 4 kilometre, to 10 kilometre, to 15 kilometre- runs. I have never been close to first over the line—usually by the time I finish most of the other competitors are at home washing their gear—but every time I do it I celebrate how far I have come.

I enrolled in a range of boot camps filled with personal trainers and freakishly fit exercise junkies. It was no surprise I found myself struggling to keep up and always came last while the others did push-ups waiting for me to arrive—usually about three or four hours later. It's hard to throw away your pride, suck it up and do it for the final outcome.

Honouring a surprisingly sober New Year's resolution, I joined a competitive women's second division soccer team after 30 years of avoiding anything involving a uniform. There had never ever been an 'I' in 'team' unless it was 'I am buying the round of drinks', so this was a big one for me.

At the time I was still fairly overweight, so they did the smartest thing and put me in goals. I discovered I was actually quite good—bit hard getting the ball past someone taking up the entire space between the posts. First division asked me to play keeper for them, but I longed to play out on the field with my sisters. I had my sights set on being one of those girls—the fit, fast ones running around for 90 minutes straight, sharing in the glory of a goal scored. So I changed to a bigger club, went down a couple of divisions and learned how to play, earning my time on the field, proving myself game by game. I discovered something else about my new self: I was a natural defender (read: aggressive), more than capable of holding my own, very competitive and I loved being part of a team.

Five years on I became a dedicated soccer mum and even found myself coaching my son's team. Who would have thought this Sporty Spice lived inside me?

Never standing still for long, I decided to push myself one step further and do something I would never have thought possible, least of all when I was well over 100 kilos, confined to a wheelchair and unable to lift my own body weight up the stairs.

I decided to do triathlons. To date I have entered more than a dozen of them of varying in distance. I am most proud of my 'big one'; I swam 1 kilometre, cycled 20 kilometres and ran 10 kilometres. I had no idea if I could actually make it all the way, but I just sucked it up and became the little engine that could.

Once again it came as no surprise that in a field of 500 people I came last or, as I like to say, first at the back end. When I looked at the times posted on the Internet, my heart is thrilled to see my name on a list of competitors in, of all things, a triathlon!

I don't care about coming last because I realise that every step I take is one more step away from the obese girl I used to be. In my pursuit of a healthy life I have learned it does not matter what you do, how you do it, how well you do it or whether you came first or last. What matters is that you are doing something that challenges you and causes you to step outside your comfort zone.

There's no limit to the things you can do, no limit to what you can discover, no limit to the challenges you set yourself. Dare to dream because you can achieve anything you set your mind to.

# Five-Minute Workouts

**I always relied on the 'I'm a single mum and can't get out of the house or afford a personal trainer' excuse to not achieve my goals. One day I decided I was sick of listening to that rubbish. I created an exercise buffer zone around my house.**

I would put Kai down for a day sleep while already dressed in my gym gear. I took the baby monitor and ran four houses each way. In between each lap I would use my front yard, stairs and fence as my workout equipment. Forty-five minutes later I was drenched in sweat and happy to have saved myself a hundred dollars in personal training fees.

Sit down and write out a series of exercises you can run through at home, in your local park or in the gym, without having to stress about what you should do next. Break your workouts into five minute increments. Every time your kids are amused for five minutes, attack one set of exercises on your list.

For example, give your kids a bowl of chopped-up fruit and some skewers and let them make fruit kebabs while you do a series of sit-ups, push-ups and squats for as long as they stay amused. Then give them coloring in to do: time for another five-minute workout, this time attacking your abs. Get them a tub of warm sudsy water and some plastic toys and you have another little block of time on your hands. Use TV ad time to do a quick five and you don't even need to leave the room.

Chances are you will find quite a few pockets of time during a day, and if you add that up it will go towards making a change for the better. Calories are burned just as well if you spread exercise out and it is better than the nothing you have previously done.

Here are a few examples of what you can do. Why not do one now?

1.

5 x sit-ups
5 x push-ups
5 x squats
5 x star jumps
5 x lunges (on each leg)

2.

5 x 30 second horizontal hovers (break them up with the other sets)
5 x burpees
5 x sit-ups
5 x triceps dips
5 x push-ups

3.

Canned food workout (use two tins of baked beans or small weights if at the gym).
5 x bicep curls
5 x sit-ups (holding the weights to your chest)
5 x boxing punches
5 x push-ups
5 x triceps curls

4.

5 x lunges
5 x squats
5 x karate kicks
5 x burpees
5 x star jumps

5.

5 x sit-ups
5 x push-ups
5 x sit-ups
5 x push-ups
5 x 30 second hovers

If you are rolling your eyes and saying 'it's only five minutes at a time' think of this: one hundred cents saved make a dollar so every second you invest in your health will give you a longer, healthier happier life.

# CELEBRATION HANGOVER

**It happens slowly. You have a series of events to go to and at first you do all right. You maintain your weight loss focus, but one little treat turns to another, you indulge a little, then a little more and before you know it your common sense filter has switched off altogether.**

This is not technically bingeing, but it is a destructive pattern of behaviour that will lead to self-hatred.

The effects of a 'celebration hangover' can manifest in many ways. For me it was the overwhelming sense of self-loathing. Worse still was the feeling of helplessness: once again weight loss seemed impossible.

Wake up! And if you wake up feeling crap do something about it! That's all you can do: something, anything, whatever it takes. It really is that simple.

There will always be times in life when you overindulge, overeat and overdrink. That is life, and these are days of decadence.

The key to healthy living is to make sure these days of decadence do not steamroll into everyday life.

Learning how to get back to healthy living as soon as possible is an important lesson, and will ensure that a couple of bad days won't ruin all your hard work.

Call it refocus, call it rediscovery, call it whatever you want, but know that it is just part of your life. So get over it and get on with it!

Know that the sooner you restart the sooner the changes will be apparent. If you don't start you won't get there.

# Mental Workouts

'Would you like me to give you a formula for success?
It's quite simple really. Double your rate of failure!'

Thomas J Watson, founder of IBM

# WHO ARE YOU?

**Are you fat?**

Are you dumpy, plain, beefy, big, blimpish, bovine, brawny, broad, bulging, bulky, bullish, burly, chubby, chunky, disgusting, dumpy, elephantine, fleshy, floppy, gargantuan, gross, heavy, hefty, hideous, hopeless or inadequate?

Are you full of lard, large, lazy, meaty, morbidly obese, old, oversized, overweight, pathetic, paunchy, plump, plumpish, porcine, portly, potbellied, pudgy, repugnant, revolting, rotund, saggy, solid, stout, stretch-marked, swollen, thickset, ugly, unfit, unhealthy, unworthy, useless, weighty, or worthless?

Seriously? Come on!

Why spend so much energy on words that weigh you down?

Think again.

You are a beautiful human being with a heart and soul worthy of dignity, honesty, hope, happiness, fulfilment, love and respect. You deserve to love and be loved. You deserve the best life can deliver you, your dreams deserve to be followed and fulfilled—your life is meant to be lived!

Be YOU! Beautiful YOU! Inside AND out!

KNOW who you REALLY are, and become ALL that you can be.

Be YOU! Now step up and become all that you can be!

Your new life begins NOW!

# FINDING YOUR ANGEL WITHIN

**Michelangelo was asked how he managed to carve such exquisite statues from a simple square of marble.**

He said, 'I saw the angel within and simply chipped away at her until she revealed herself to me.'

My trainer used to tell me that the body of a goddess was already within me. She was covered by a velvety curtain of fat, but each time I went for a run that curtain would rise a little higher, until eventually she was revealed.

You too have a beautiful angel within, and you are the artist that shapes her. All of your efforts will chip away at the stone, ultimately revealing your healthier self.

Imagine if Michelangelo had looked at those huge blocks of marble and said, 'You know what? My statue of David is a great idea but honestly, it's just too hard. My hands will hurt and probably bleed from the repeated beating of the chisel against stone. My body will ache from the hours I have to put in to get it even close to looking like a man, let alone a great work of art. It might take me a whole year or more. Surely the whole piece will be ruined if I have a bad day and do something wrong.'

It is better to focus on what you can do now, rather than how long it will take or how hard it will be to get to your goal. Every strike of that chisel is one that brings the artist closer to their masterpiece.

It is your hand that will create the final picture. Whether that hand is going to your mouth or whether it is driving you to the gym, you are the artist and you have within you all it takes to make it happen.

Now go out there and empower yourself with every step you take, because each little fleck of chipped stone is one that comes closer to revealing the angel within.

# Every Thought Flies

**I recently walked the Great Wall of China for Olivia Newton John's charity, along with many cancer survivors, people who had lost loved ones and a whole bunch of celebrity ring-ins. We aimed to raise enough money to build a state-of-the-art cancer research and treatment hospital.**

A day or two into the walk a few people caught the flu, and before we knew it one of our two buses was constantly filled with an ever-evolving group of ill people. We jokingly renamed the buses Bus A (for "I am A OK") and Bus B (for "Bacteria Bus"). Everyone on that trip ended up on Bus B at some point—except for me.

I do NOT subscribe to the 's' word ('sick'). Whenever someone mentioned the flu or sneezed in my direction, I would loudly declare to anyone who was listening (and many who were not), 'I am healthy, strong and immune.' When people asked how I was at breakfast, I proudly said, 'I'm good thanks, I am healthy, strong and immune, how are you?'

I repeated this mantra constantly for fourteen days, until it went from being mildly hilarious to very annoying for everyone else. Whenever I felt a slight twinge in my throat or the tiniest bit of a runny nose, I said the magic words over and over, and within hours the symptoms would disappear. I was the only person who did NOT get sick on that trip.

I say this mantra every day upon waking and again when going to sleep. I continue to use it whenever anyone around me speaks of illness and I continue to be healthy, strong and immune.

Many who have beaten serious illness will tell you it is the power of positive thinking they turned to first. Give power to the thoughts that fly and do not for a second entertain those that bring you down.

# Know That You Are Wonderful

**Sometimes we put so much value on the size of our thighs we forget that inside of us there is a beautiful human being with plenty to feel good about.**

When the scales send you into a spin, or you are frustrated that you are just not 'there' yet, don't turn to chocolate for a tasty but weighty hug. Do this little exercise instead.

Take five minutes out of your day right now and email five friends. Ask them to indulge you for just a few minutes, promise you will never send those stupid chain emails again if they spare you some time and energy now.

Ask your friends to email you with your five best qualities. Print out the replies and stick them on your fridge, because if you are anything like me that is the first place you turn to 'feel good' about yourself. Frame them, decorate them, stick them beside your bed or over your desk.

It's a simple reminder that you are a beautiful person and deserve the very best in life, with or without success on the scales.

# WHAT'S INSIDE YOU?

**For most of my life I would wake and find myself stuck in a body I hated. One day, with the help of my trainer, I decided to think differently.**

When I hit a plateau, my trainer told me to try and connect with the body I was creating. She said it was already there, hidden under the fat. It was incredibly powerful to be told that the body I wanted was not separate from me.

Instead of running my hands over the fat I wanted to be rid of, I learned to close my eyes and visualise the powerful, sensual, fit body inside me. After all, it was mine already.

I imagined that I was a doll in a jar packed with cotton balls. Every time I exercised and ate well I imagined myself physically removing one of the cotton wool balls.

It's taken a while, but I now automatically have positive thoughts about the potential I carry in my body. When I find maintenance challenging I simply remind myself that I am already the person I want to be. It's like tricking yourself into fitness.

In the mornings, try spending an extra five minutes in bed actively visualising your fit, healthy, sexy body. Think how much you love getting fit and choosing healthy foods. Remember that your hot new bod is already inside of you, just waiting to be released from all that cotton wool!

# THE MIRROR IS YOUR FRIEND...

**It's easy to avoid mirrors when you have put on weight. It's time to think differently and use them to your advantage.**

Go to a gym with lots of mirrors and look at yourself. Be proud that you are changing, and know that in one month's time you will look different.

Instead of getting depressed about your fat wobbling as you exercise, watch it in the mirror and think that with every little jiggle it is actually shaking its way off you.

For every cringing moment, channel that energy into action. Say to yourself, 'I love that view because it reminds me of the changes I am making now!' This person in the mirror will soon be gone, and you will never have to look at that fat again.

# Dance Like No-one is Watching

**While on holiday in Fiji, Kai and I decided to hike up to a waterfall. It was an easy hike up the mountain, but very long and hot. The sight of a cool, safe and exhilaratingly fresh waterfall was so welcome it took us all of three seconds to throw off our shorts and dive into the water. It was even more fun to climb to the top of the rocks and swing off the rope into the middle of the natural blue pool.**

After about fifteen minutes I realised that we were the only ones swimming, apart from the local kids. I noticed the people sitting it out were all overweight. I remembered being the person who didn't take part and I felt sad for them. I was glad that I had healed myself, and because of that my son and I both had a better quality of life.

Don't be one of those people who watches other people live. Be the parent playing in the park with her kids, or swinging off the rope at the waterfall. Be the person you want to be. Push fear aside, let your heart grow wings and do whatever you can today to live a better life NOW.

# ART THERAPY

**What creative activity makes your heart happy? Is it scrapbooking, pottery, jewellery making, painting…or maybe you dreamed of making your own clothes but never got around to it?**

Take the money you have spent on sweets and alcohol. Take the money you would previously throw away on takeaway. Spend a month not eating out and use that money too. Now you have a great little nest egg to invest in your art.

Those idle hours you would have spent sitting on the couch eating food you don't need, or drinking your nights away, can be spent making beautiful jewellery or paintings for your home. Who knows, maybe you will discover an untapped talent—you never know how far it could take you. You could sell handmade trinkets at your local markets, start a scrapbooking business or end up the next big thing on Project Runway.

It's amazing how one small ripple can become the wave of change that truly transforms your life.

# Letting Go to Grow

**Warning: the following message may be considered a little bit 'hippy'.**

Success is more about your state of mind than what you do on any given day. You need to be a blank canvas, freshly primed, ready to fulfil all of your potential. Yesterday is old news. Today and tomorrow is all that you have. You don't need a lobotomy to start fresh; all you need to do is teach yourself to let go.

This is one of my favourite mental exercises. It is easy and the more you do it the better it gets.

Run a bath and fill it with Epsom salts. Epsom salts' fancy name is magnesium sulphate, which is absorbed through the skin. It draws toxins from the body, sedates the nervous system, reduces swelling, relaxes muscles, is a natural emollient, great for exfoliating and much more. Basically, it's good stuff and you should have a big bag of it in your bathroom cupboard.

Set the scene. Light candles, burn some incense and put on some relaxing music. As you enter the bath, acknowledge that you are entering a new, healthy, happy phase of your life. In water you are embracing weightlessness.

While you lie there, think about all the things in your life that have made you happy. Think of the times when you have felt powerful, strong, focused, in control and successful. Think of how it felt to walk with your head held high, excited by the energy and potential around you. Think of your happiest moments and let that energy course around your body. Breathe in deeply, almost like you are drinking the memory, embracing that feel good energy. As you exhale, release all the negative feelings, all the thoughts that keep you trapped in your unhappiness, all the discontent and all the bad habits.

As you take the next deep breath and fill your body with the energy of success, tell yourself this is the state you now dwell in, and this is the state you will come back to any time you find yourself slipping back into a negative thought pattern.

Repeat for as long as the bath is warm, and until the happiness fits you like a glove. When it is time to get out, pull the plug and say out loud, "I release the past. I am letting it all go.

I am free. I am focused and energised by my future, and nothing else matters. I am happy. I am energised. I am powerful. I am successful. I now choose to live in a constant state of manifesting my potential. I let go of all that I used to be to become all that I am.' I always like to add my own personal touch with, 'I am on fire!'

Go to bed content, and think only about the positive. As soon as negative thoughts cross your mind, banish them and relive the memories of feeling happy, successful and powerful. Bring that energy into your life now.

When you wake up in the morning, take five minutes to dwell on that energy again. Talk yourself through how great your day is going to be, how you will overcome obstacles with hope and determination and how grateful you are to be moving forward to success. Be excited to face the challenges that enable you to learn and grow, and feel inspired by constantly dwelling in a happy, empowered state.

Then get out of bed and seize the day. It is all yours for the taking!

# Practise Happiness

**If you are caught in a funk, how the heck do you get yourself out it?**

Happiness is contagious and you are about to spread an epidemic of it.

When I was overweight I was grumpy and miserable, and I lashed out at anyone who got in my way. I was looking for an outlet for my disappointment and anger; if I could not be happy then I didn't want anyone else to be. What a selfish little bore I had become.

Without even realising it, I would walk around sighing with my shoulders slumped. My language was always negative. No wonder I found myself obese and alone, my only friend a triple chocolate cheesecake.

I had a friend who was always positive, loving, smiling and laughing. She would bounce around life, and everyone always wanted to spend time with her or bend over backwards to help her. She naturally attracted happiness.

One day, I tried 'happiness' on for size and found it absolutely transformed my life.

I remembered times in my life when I was happiest and lived in that state. I asked sales people how their day was going like I meant it, I patted dogs and said hello to their owners, I opened doors for the elderly with joy in my heart, gave up my seat with a smile to ladies with babies, and I sent love and light to everyone.

Doors opened, faces broke open with smiles, telephone operators tried to help me and suddenly, so much of my day was better and so much of my heart happier that I didn't feel the need to eat to be happy. My social life improved, my business relationships got better and my career hit new heights.

It's that same old 'bluff it till you become it', but this works straight away. Buddha said, 'If you can fix it, don't worry about it. If you can't fix it then don't worry about it.' So don't worry about it. Just be happy for the sake of happiness. See how many people it affects. You are a smiling virus and incredibly infections. Heal yourself, your heart, and your life with happiness one better day at a time because best of all—it's free!

# FEED THE MIND FIRST

**Mind, body and spirit: all three need to be balanced and healthy for us to operate effectively. There is no point being stick thin if your only fuel is fear. How much love will you have for others if you are consumed with self-loathing?**

You need to find whatever is missing in your life. Become spirit-rich. Work yourself into such a state of happiness and contentment that you have no need to sabotage your goals. When you are in a positive state of mind you will naturally treat yourself better. When you treat yourself well you naturally attract a more positive state of mind. It's the not-so-vicious circle.

You don't have to don sandals and robes and trek across India to find peace. There are many ways to find contentment and calm in your daily travels: motivational CDs and DVDs, meditation, self-hypnosis, life coaching … the list goes on.

I love nothing better than waking up to an inspirational track on my iPod. Later in the day I nana-nap for 45 minutes with a self-hypnosis track designed to focus my mind on success. I keep little books of wisdom everywhere I can use a quick pick-me-up.

Modern technology has made it even easier to invest in your entire self. Five minutes is all it takes to feel richer, happier and healthier in every way.

# GRATITUDE

**I was driving around in a bit of a grumble: 'I don't get paid enough. I can't find a babysitter, This person did this to me. I can't believe this person said that about me. I wish I owned my own home. Why don't I have the perfect body? Why is life so hard on me?'**

Then I stopped at the traffic lights and I saw a lady in a wheelchair that had gotten stuck on the incline up onto the footpath. I pulled the car over, got out and pushed her up so she could keep going on her way as she walked her dog. 'Bless you,' she said. Bless me? My God, what a wake-up call for my stupid selfish thoughts. Bless her, please.

Be grateful. Be happy. Work hard and set goals, but be thankful for what you DO have right now, and for being aware enough and capable enough for change.

Today I am grateful for a healthy life full of promise, a son who is healthy, happy, vibrant and finding his way in a world that is often confusing and confronting for him, and a school that accepts him for who he is. I have a roof over my head, contact with women who inspire me every day and I am alive.

I am grateful that I have sight and breath and hearing and a body that is not debilitated. I have a mind that works, a heart that is full, hands that touch and feel and a soul that strives to create a better life.

I am not perfect and I am thankful for the lessons I receive daily in humility, love, compassion, strength, hope and gratitude.

*'Do not be anything but what you are, and try to be that perfectly.'*

# Someone Else's Shoes

**It is unreasonable to assume that every person can manifest all the inspiration they need to achieve all their dreams just like that. If that was the case then** *The Secret* **would not have sold fifty bajillion copies, and every person walking the planet would have everything they ever desired without having to try.**

Being smart is accepting that you may not have all the answers you need. Aquiring knowledge is a never-ending process and education is available to everyone. True wisdom is being brave enough to seek the truth. Greatness is learning how to turn mistakes into the stepping stones to success.

There have been so many inspirational people of our time. Even if you can't afford to buy your heroes' biographies, there is more than enough information on the Internet to constantly find a reason to keep going when the times are tough. Accessing your local public library is almost as good as hiring Lance Armstrong as your personal trainer.

Google your heroes or those who do the sports you are interested in. Find what made them get out of bed in the morning; learn the tricks they used to overcome fear, failure, fatigue and everyday distractions; get inside their heads, spend time in someone else's shoes and take what inspiration you need to do the same with your life. Sure, you may not be going for gold, but your goal of living a healthier, happier life is just as important as an Olympian's.

# Truly Beautiful. Are You?

**It is so easy to fall into the mechanism of 'reasoning' why you should feel bad about your body, or why you have fallen into a funk and won't pull yourself out of it (notice I didn't say 'can't get out of it!').**

I think I was in one of those 'I can't go out because I've got nothing to wear' phases when I met this awesome woman who challenged all my previous concepts of beauty. She was born with a condition called craniofacial disfigurement. She has not even celebrated her 21st birthday and already she has had five major reconstructions to her face and major surgery to her brain. She endured years of cruel teasing at school, survived years of life-threatening, painful surgeries and has spent her life having people stare, point and make inappropriate comments.

She is one of the most beautiful women I have ever been fortunate enough to meet. I only spent 20 minutes with her but my day was brighter and better for it. She talked about how kids had teased her at school, and how she learned to look deeper into them and see what makes even a bully beautiful inside. How she could come to that conclusion I don't know, but it represents the loving beautiful spirit that she is.

She then went on to quote the Dalai Lama, who says if you can't be nice about someone then say nothing at all. She said she learnt to turn negative thoughts away. Instead of hating people she just thought nothing of them, or even felt pity that they could not see the inner beauty of others.

This woman has gone on to found her own charity called Truly Beautiful. She raises money and provides support for other girls in situations such as hers. She provides anti-bullying lectures, support and counselling. She guides young women to finding and believing in their own true beauty. She gives them strength to grow beyond other people's ugliness, prejudice and small mindedness.

Ironically enough, after all her facial reconstructions this young woman is incredibly beautiful on the outside as well. You could not guess how much she has gone through. She says it is tragic that women judge their happiness by the number on a scale and I cannot help but agree with her.

On those days when you say you couldn't be bothered because you are just so depressed about size of your thighs, spare a thought for people like this. Then get off your arse and go for a walk; set yourself some healthy eating guidelines; shave your legs; help a friend; do something for someone else or even just love yourself exactly as you are. Then get yourself sorted and live every precious second of life you have in the best way possible.

We are all truly blessed and we are all truly beautiful, and we have everything we need to live life exactly as we want. You just have to make the effort.

# STEP OUTSIDE YOUR COMFORT ZONE

**I grew up doing ballet, jazz and tap. I never had the stick insect body required to become a professional dancer but I loved it anyway. As an adult I continued classes, but when I became anorexic I barely had the energy to get out of bed. Then when I moved into the land of the bulimic and my butt grew to the size of a circus elephant's, I stopped dancing and acting all together and entered ten years of misery and unhealthy living.**

Going back to dance classes was the one thing I was going to do when I got to my perfect weight. When I finally made it to the mid-70 kilos mark, however, I realised there is no such thing as the perfect weight and that it was dumb to be waiting to have fun. I could continue to half live my life according to my weight or I could step outside my comfort zone and embrace what I loved to do.

Heart beating wildly, I looked at my cottage cheese thighs and hoped the dancers didn't dip their crackers into me in the hope of getting a feed. Then I realised dancers don't eat so my thighs were safe. I swallowed my pride, donned my tracky daks and joggers and went to beginner's jazz.

The room must have had at least 80 people in it. I hid up the back and was surprised to see women almost twice my age, and some the size I was when I started my weight loss journey. I silently high-fived those girls and marvelled at their bravery.

The class started and the warm-ups were simple—anyone could do them. I held my head a little higher; I wasn't that bad after all. I sneakily pushed my way through to the middle of the room.

The class moved on and we learnt the routine. This is where it all started to unravel. The teacher was one of the guys I had danced with ten years ago and he hadn't aged a bit. It was like some weird scene from *Death Becomes Her*. Had he sold his soul to the devil when I had sold mine to Colonel Sanders? I prayed he wouldn't recognise me.

Just then, as everyone did a double pirouette and I did what could only be described as an upright belly flop closely followed by a body roll, the teacher did a double take. 'Ajay?' he asked. I wanted to run and hide. I wanted to say, 'no, my name's Sarah Jane Smith and I've never heard of an Ajay.' Instead I tripped trying to do the next step, lost my place and tried to act like I wasn't having a heart attack.

It didn't matter in the end. He didn't care. I'd always been fat in dancer terms (which incidentally is not fat at all). Whatever, I reminded myself, at least I am doing something about it. At least I am doing something I love. At least I am actually living my life rather than waiting for my weight to be perfect.

In the end I had a ball. I laughed a lot, mostly because I couldn't get the steps, and when I did everyone was already three steps ahead of me. It didn't matter. I was growing as a person.

I love dancing and try to go to as many classes as I can. I always walk out skipping to my car, a little bit taller, a good deal happier and maybe even a little bit thinner—and it doesn't matter if I'm not, because I am living my life to the fullest.

Step outside your comfort zone. You will be amazed at what you can do and who you can be. Dare to be all that you have ever wanted to be and if all else fails: bluff it until you become it!

# BE KIND TO YOURSELF

*Forgive yourself.*

*Speak kindly to yourself.*

*Love yourself.*

*Know that by doing your best, you are doing all you can for now.*

*Every minute of every day is an opportunity to start fresh.*

*Every minute of every day is a chance to change your life for the better forever.*

*Every minute you devote to getting healthy is time you add to your life.*

*Every change you make NOW is a diet you don't have to go on in the future.*

*The changes you make NOW are changes you will never have to make again.*

*You deserve the very best life has to offer.*

*Believe you can make the change and make the change NOW!*

*This is forever.*

*This is for life.*

*This is for a better life.*

# Random Acts of Charity

**How many times did your mother say to you, 'there are a million kids in Africa starving to death that would be happy for that meal, now eat it.'? Forget that she was serving you enough to food to satisfy an entire African village. Sometimes we really have our priorities confused. It's not too late to do your bit.**

Are you one of those people who cooks too much and 'saves the rest for leftovers', and then the uneaten meal sits in the fridge until it becomes a scientific study? Why don't you cut down the size of the meals you make by half, and see how it impacts on your shopping bill? Then you can satisfy your stomach, your desire to shrink your waist and indulge your mother's misplaced charitable thoughts by actually donating that extra money to charity.

You do not have to lock yourself into a month-by-month contract to save the world. World Vision has a great program where a one-off payment, when you can afford it, can buy a soccer ball for a kid, or a chicken and a goat for a village. You would be amazed at the difference one goat or one chicken can make (feathers, eggs, more chickens, meat and fertiliser).

And what about the oversized meals we are served at restaurants? How many times has a doggy bag not even been given to the dog? I eat small meals whether it is at home or dining out. However, with an almost-teenaged and very athletic (read: hungry) boy in tow I usually have to order two adult meals. That generally leaves me with some pretty decent leftovers that I really don't need to eat the next day or ever.

Think about having that extra food packaged up into one or two takeaway bags. Then, on the way home keep your eyes peeled for someone less fortunate than you and offer them the food (I've never had anyone refuse). Sadly you really don't have to travel too far to find someone homeless and hungry, who on any other day would be rifling through that back alley bin for a meal.

I know this is controversial and not everyone will agree with me, but I have been hungry AND homeless so I understand the value in a random act of charity. If you saw the eyes of a hungry person when you offered them good, hot, fresh food in a nice clean container, then you would never leave a table full of food behind again.

# PAMPER YOURSELF

**There's nothing like a bit of pampering to get you out of the dumps. You will feel better about yourself, which in turn will help you make healthier choices in your day-to-day life.**

Ajay's hotlist of self pampering

1. Moisturise your whole body, morning and night (The Body Shop's mango body butter is divine).

2. Put day and night cream on your face and eyes.

3. Use heel balm on your feet every night.

4. Give yourself a foot spa and pedicure.

5. Paint your nails.

6. Shave your legs and anywhere else that might need it.

7. Whiten your teeth.

8. Give yourself a hair treatment.

9. Exfoliate your whole body.

10. Use a pumice stone on your feet.

11. Get a fake tan.

12. Put lip balm on before going to bed.

13. Brush your hair 100 times daily.

14. Keep a diary.

15. Take a ten-minute break. Sit down, have a cup of tea and listen to one song that makes your heart sing.

16. Pluck your eyebrows.

17. Give yourself a mud-pack facial.

18.  Have a bubble bath. To make it even more special, use a sparkle bath bomb.

19.  Take yourself out to a picnic lunch. Eat a yummy homemade salad and then relax with a good book.

20.  Give yourself a manicure.

Remind yourself you deserve the best every single day of your life.

# THE HEALING POWER OF LAUGHTER

**We never laughed much in my household growing up. With regular beatings from an abusive mother and an alcoholic father, there really wasn't a lot to laugh about. The closest I came to ever seeing anything funny was reading out the jokes in the Christmas crackers. I used to collect them and paste them in my diary, returning to them every night for a break in a life.**

I remember hearing this amazing story of survival from a friend of mine around the age of sixteen, and I have never ever forgotten it.

Rob* was my best friend's dad. He had played rugby for Australia and was a national hero before my friend was born.

One day, not long after his illustrious career had come to an end, Rob was diagnosed with testicular cancer and given only a few months to live. As the doctors put it: 'A few weeks to go home, tie up loose ends, say goodbye to his loved ones and die.'

Well, Rob was having none of it. He decided he was going to live and beat the cancer. He booked himself into chemo, but also took his healing into his own hands. He had read that laughter was the best medicine, and he was going to prove that it was so.

Rob, a part-time graphic artist in his new career, made up lots of signs for his hospital room and badges for the nurses to wear. They said, 'A laugh a day keeps the cancer away.' When anyone came into his room they first had to tell him a joke. He even had joke books pinned to the door. As the cancer became more aggressive so did his own attack, with funny hats and silly masks hanging from a coat rack, which doctors and nurses had to don before coming in to treat him.

Visits with family members were raucous occasions, a room filled with howls of laughter and many tears, not of sadness but of absolute hilarity. They brought in tales to share with him in the desperate hope it would save their dad. The doctors didn't believe and treated him like a dying man, but his family gave him everything because hope and miracles were all they had left.

Did it work?

A few years ago I watched a video of this now sixty-year-old man celebrate his birthday by competing in, and winning, his age category in the Gold Coast Iron Man event. Thirty years ago, his cancer inexplicably disappeared, to never return again.

Next time someone asks you why the chicken crossed the road, don't roll your eyes. Embrace the joke and heal your life! Anything is possible and if this man can cure himself of cancer, then you can cure yourself of obesity.

* Not his real name

# TOILET TRAINING

**I completely believe that if we tell ourselves something often enough we will become it. Language is our energy and what we say becomes our reality.**

I once called myself a big girl in a big world, and I stayed that way till it nearly killed me. One day I started calling myself a triathlete, even though I was far from it. That did not stop me from adapting the language and lifestyle of an athlete 'in training'.

What has that to do with toilet training? Like most people, I spend a bit of time in my bathroom and I like to put that quiet time to good use and retrain my brain.

The changes I am making determine what goes on the door of my toilet, written on my mirror or taped to the glass door of my shower (taped to the outside and laminated).

When I was 'becoming an athlete', these were the mantras I had taped to my toilet door:

*My first priority of the day is exercise, because I'm in training!*

*When I wake up I drink two whole glasses of water to flush my system, because I'm in training!*

*I eat only healthy, fresh food, because I'm in training!*

*When I work out I work as hard as I possibly can, because I'm in training!*

*I only eat food that furthers my goals, because I'm in training!*

*I regularly refuel my body with healthy wholesome food, because I'm in training!*

*I log everything I eat to ensure I am giving myself the best possible chance of achieving my goals, because I'm in training!*

*For the next little while I will stay home more often: I have greater priorities than drinking with friends or eating fatty food, because I'm in training!*

*Every night before sleep I spend fifteen minutes visualising my training and my ever-changing body. I spend time planning my meals and my day so I can achieve all my goals, because I'm in training!*

*At the beginning of every week I set new goals, because I'm in training!*

*At the end of each week I honestly assess how I have done with my goals and make changes to ensure next week will be even better, because I'm in training!*

*When people try to lure me on a different path to the one I have chosen, I feel pity that they cannot grasp the concept that I am not dieting, I'm in training!*

*Everyday I feel empowered because with each healthy choice I inch closer to achieving the life and body I have always dreamed of. Everyday I become more and more connected with the freedom of being healthy and the knowledge that I am, in fact, in training!*

*When I train I push myself further, faster, harder because every step I take outside my normal routine will take me one step closer to becoming the athletic person I am striving to be.*

*Nothing tastes better than the taste of success.*

*I will buy wet weather gear because I will not allow the elements to get in the way of the fact that I'm in training!*

*I am focused, dedicated and excited by the fact that I am in training!*

*I am in training!*

Every day I read these goals. I whispered them to myself in the morning and shouted them out in the shower at night. Every time someone asked me out to dinner or to a party I replied, 'I can't because I am in training!' I said it with gusto and belief and ignored that terrified-fat-girl-afraid-of-the-world voice that tried to tell me there was no way I could do a triathlon. 'In training' meant I was already there. I saw the finish line, I ran over it in my mind a thousand times. It was not just my body but also my mind and spirit that was 'in training'. It takes all three to get you there.

People laughed at my repetitive 'play-acting' statements, but let me tell you, when I crossed the finish line of my very first triathlon, I knew I would never be that fat girl driving down the street to buy bread again.

I was no longer 'in training'—I had become someone else. Or, really, just a better me!

Use your space to help you focus—walls, doors, car, bathroom, bedside table, wallet, work desk. Put inspiring books and motivational quotes within your reach, write signs and goalposts everywhere, read them and ultimately become them. It doesn't matter what anyone thinks of the methods you employ to get what you want. You are free to be whoever, however and whatever you want.

# What's Your Excuse?

**I have heard a million of them. 'I have a bad back. I had an accident a few years ago. I'm just not athletic."**

You are only limited by the limitations you put on yourself.

There are some people who look adversity in the eye and find even more reasons to follow their dreams.

**What's your excuse?**

Aimee Mullins was born with fibular hemimelia, a limb anomaly where there is partial or total absence of the shinbones. She had both legs amputated below the knee when she was only a year old. Her amazing spirit and drive helped compensate for the portion of her body that was missing.

Despite her physical limitations, she pushed herself physically and mentally to succeed. In high school she participated in numerous sports, including softball and skiing. She competed against 'able-bodied' athletes.

She attended Georgetown University, where she became the first disabled athlete to compete in the National Collegiate Athletic Association (NCAA) Division 1 track and field.

At the Paralympic Games trials, she ran so fast she was placed with arm amputees at the following meet instead, without being told. She finished last, and though she was upset, it didn't stop her. She set Paralympic records in Atlanta for the 100- and 200-metre dash and in the long jump.

The following year she was named USA Track and Field's Disabled Athlete of the Year, and the National Association of Women in Education's 1997 Woman of Distinction.

She remains active in sports and served as 2005's president-elect of the Women's Sports Foundation, a 'charitable educational organisation dedicated to advancing the lives of girls and women through sports and physical activity.'

'Confidence is the sexiest thing a woman can have. It's much sexier than any body part.'
Aimee Mullins, *O Magazine*, May 2004

## What's your excuse?

Thirteen-year-old surfer Bethany Hamilton lost her arm in a shark attack but never lost her faith, or her love of surfing. Bethany began her surfing career with her first competition at the age of 11. By the age of 13, she was riding the waves at the top of her sport.

Her lifelong dream was to become a professional surfer. But on October 31, 2003, that dream was nearly shattered when she was attacked by a 14-foot tiger shark while surfing in Hawaii. Calmly, she pushed the pain aside and began to paddle with one arm, taking the time and effort to alert other surfers of the danger lurking in the water. She was rushed to hospital and after surgery the first thing Bethany wanted to know was, "when can I surf again?"

Just three weeks after the incident, she returned to her board and went surfing again. Initially, she adopted a custom-made board that was longer and slightly thicker which made it easier to paddle. After teaching herself to surf with one arm, she has again begun surfing competitively. She is now back to using performance short-boards again.

In July 2004 Bethany won the ESPY award for Best Comeback Athlete of the Year.

In 2005, with one arm, she took first place in the NSSA National Championships, a goal she had been trying to achieve since before the shark attack. In 2008, she began competing full-time in the (ASP) World Qualifying Series (WQS). In her first competition against many of the world's best women surfers, she finished third.

In 2004, MTV Books published Hamilton's book, Soul Surfer: A True Story of Faith, Family, and Fighting to Get Back on the Board. She continues to surf and inspire others to follow their dreams despite how impossible and improbable they may be.

## What's your excuse?

The human spirit, when it desires something strongly enough, can overcome any obstacle put in its way. Do not tell yourself why you cannot do something, instead ask how you can.

Now go and make your dreams come true!

# Ask and You Shall Receive

**I've always believed in the power of personal manifestation, recently made popular with books such as *The Secret*. Sometimes I have had a little fun with it, most recently during my annual holiday in Fiji.**

I travel with another family who have two children the same age as my son Kai. One day we put the kids in kids club and decided to circumnavigate this idyllic tropical island. It hadn't looked too big in the brochures and had beautiful white sandy beaches where the resort was. So, in hindsight rather foolishly, we set off on what we thought would be a few hours of a walking adventure, just like the brochures promised.

It started off okay. We turned two points and continued on what looked like kilometre stretches of tropical perfection. Not realising the island had about six points (a kind of misshapen star and not the heart shape we thought it was), it was not until we passed the third point that we thought we might have issues. The beach was long, and towards the end there was dense scrub and what looked to be a rocky point. We passed our one and only person who looked to be a long-term expat local. He had skin like leather and looked a little like Tom Hanks in *Castaway*. Worried about the time it would now take us (we had to be back in three hours to get the kids) we asked him how far along we were.

He pointed along the beach and explained most people cut through the coconut plantation and were back though to the resort in no time at all. He looked at us a little strangely when we explained we were doing the whole island. He shrugged his shoulders and walked off after telling us we should do it in less than three hours. He also wished us good luck.

We passed the path back to the resort and proceeded to the part of the beach we couldn't see from the other end. For good reason: there was no more beach, just a huge Rocky Balboa cliffhanger-type rock face. It's probably at this point I should mention we were dressed in swimmers, sarongs, bare feet and cameras: not so good for climbing cliff faces. We waded out into the sea, only to walk over sharp rocks and coral, slipping and cutting ourselves, bleeding into the ocean. I tried to stave of my all-consuming fear of shark attack.

We decided to swim for about 200 metres and ended up on a beach of busted up coral, not a grain of soft pearly white sand anywhere. Cut, bleeding and with stone bruises all over our feet, I stopped limping, raised my face towards heaven and said, 'I need some shoes. Universe, please send me some thongs as I can't go on without them.'

Three steps later one of my friends laughingly picked up a kid's thong and handed it to me. It fit (only just) and I limped on. With one foot looked after I yelled out, 'Universe I need another please.' Ten more steps and there was another thong sitting amongst the coral and driftwood. Problem was it was another left foot. And so I said, 'Sorry universe, I meant a shoe for the right foot please.'

My friends had a good old laugh when, in a few more steps, there were four right-footed shoes. But these were all men's crusty old joggers. And so I said, 'Sorry universe. Can I please have a clean right-footed thong?'

I'm sure my friends thought me mad but within a few more steps there it was, waiting for me to come get it. It was the polar opposite to the tiny child's one I was wearing: a jumbo man-sized thong. By now my friends were convinced I had truly manifested these shoes.

I spent the rest of the walk skipping ten steps ahead of my limping, barefooted friends singing to myself, 'Ask and you shall receive—but be specific!'

# Don't Get Ahead of Yourself: Why the Heck Not?

**One of my favourite movies is *Goal*. It's about a young boy who, despite his father not believing in him, follows his dreams, risks everything, and becomes a professional footballer.**

We spend so much of our lives in the shadow of our parents, sometimes trapped within the limits they have set for us. Very few of us spread our wings and dare to fly beyond the expectations of those around us, but when we do, the rewards are often great.

My mother never encouraged me to take risks. She always put me down and when I did dare to share my dreams with her, she would scoff and say, 'Don't get ahead of yourself.'

I dreamt of doing many things, some of which have never transpired. But many other ambitions I set for myself did come true, and some even more than I could have imagined. Until I am dead, there is still plenty of time to do everything I have my heart set upon. Who the heck says I won't get on *Oprah*? Who says I won't be a billionaire? Who says I can't run a marathon?

DO get ahead of yourself. Do set some damn big goals. Dreaming is free and goal setting is for people who plan to do something with their life. I once read that great minds are often met with violent opposition by mediocre minds. Every time someone laughs at the sights you set, laugh at their inability to see all the amazing opportunities that await you.

# SO YOU THINK YOU KNOW YOURSELF?

**How many times have you said, 'I have to go to the gym first thing or it just won't happen. I have loads of resolve in the mornings and then it just disappears.'**

Guess what? That is a total load of BS. You have exactly the same amount of resolve 24 hours a day.

Guess what? You, as a person, will never actually change.

Guess what? Despite the above, you can change the way you do everything.

Guess what? You have exactly the same amount of resolve 24 hours a day.

Guess what? You have exactly the same amount of resolve at lunch time as you do in the morning.

Guess what? You have exactly the same amount of resolve after work, as you did at lunchtime, as you do in the morning. What changes is how you decide to use this resolve— whether you go the gym or give up on your goals, go home and stuff your face.

Guess what? It takes the same amount of energy to make either decision. You can put your thoughts and energy into convincing yourself to work out or you can put your thoughts and energy into convincing yourself not to work out.

But guess what? You will spend more energy beating yourself up and hating your body if you don't go for a workout than if you did.

And guess what? You would have much more energy if you actually went to the gym instead of wasting energy talking yourself out of it.

It is just as easy to decide to do it as it is to decide not to do it.

# Jumping
# Hurdles

'I never ran a thousand miles. I could never have done that. I ran one mile a thousand times.'

Stu Mittleman, world record holder for ultra-distance marathon running

# Do Not Give Up at the First Sign of Trouble

**When you say 'I've taken a step backward', what does that mean? Does it mean you have failed?**

One step backwards does not put you back where you started unless it is your very first step. Even then you will have learned something. Every single step is one in the right direction, even when you fall down.

Three steps forward and one back still equals two steps forward. You can never fail as long as you keep moving.

When you embrace the concept that falling down is an opportunity to learn, you can enjoy the journey and spend your energy moving forward rather than worrying.

Write a list of the things you will do when you 'fall down'. For example:

I will:

- ❀ Read a list of my goals out loud.
- ❀ Do something nice for myself—for example have a bath, do my nails or moisturise my body.
- ❀ Look in the mirror and admire the body that lies within.
- ❀ Go for a walk.
- ❀ Throw out the leftovers of any unhealthy food I have eaten.
- ❀ Drink some water.
- ❀ Buy myself some flowers.
- ❀ Ring a friend and ask for a pep talk.
- ❀ Try on my skinny jeans.
- ❀ Look at old photos of myself and remember how it felt to run with ease.
- ❀ Know that I can do this.
- ❀ Talk to someone who is going through the same thing.

- ❀ Remind myself that I am in control.
- ❀ Forgive myself.
- ❀ Write down what I could have done to not fall down.
- ❀ Write down how I feel after eating the food I just ate.
- ❀ Read my 'mood food diary' to remind myself how I feel when I eat healthy food.
- ❀ Remind myself of my goals.
- ❀ Never give up.

Be like the phoenix: rise out of the ashes every single time. Everything is possible. Every new day is an opportunity to do your very best.

The next step is to write out your mantras. For example:

- ❀ Just one kilo. Off forever.
- ❀ Exercise every day, even if it's just walking.
- ❀ These last few steps will make all the difference!
- ❀ Zip up those boots baby!
- ❀ Fruit for snacks. Protein to fill you up.
- ❀ Cut down your carbs.
- ❀ Just 50 sit-ups every day. Do them now. (I put this opposite my bed and do them on waking and sleeping).
- ❀ Feel like a wine? Drink water.

I print them out and stick them everywhere. The babysitters think I am mad, but I don't care—it's my house!

Just remember, falling down is not the end of the world. It is simply a chance to overcome obstacles, create new pathways and have the opportunity to succeed.

# YOU ARE EVERYTHING THAT HAS HAPPENED TO YOU AND SO MUCH MORE

**I want you to be honest with yourself.**

What is more painful?

Is it the fact that 20 years ago some pervert stole your innocence, or is it the fact that you have heart palpitations every time you walk up the stairs?

What is more painful?

Is it the fact that your sports teacher humiliated you in front of all the other kids at school, or waking up thinking how unhappy you are with your life?

What is more painful?

Is it believing you could have avoided making all the mistakes you have made, or accepting that you have let opportunities slip through your greasy fingers just because you believed you were not worthy?

What is more painful?

Is it all the hurtful things people have ever said and done to you, or the hurtful things you say and do to yourself NOW?

Let the past go—deal with it, heal it. Forgive but don't forget—all of your experiences have shaped you and given you strength to survive. Nothing else exists except right now and what you do with your future. So dream big and build high, because the pendulum is swinging upward and you are going to ride it like the wind!

# REASONS TO GET OUT OF BED ON DAYS YOU DON'T WANT TO

✿ Just because you can't see the light at the end of the tunnel does not mean it isn't there.

✿ Bedsores are not great conversation starters.

✿ Think back to the first time you had your heart broken. It wasn't easy, but aren't you glad you aren't married to them now with seventeen kids, a triple mortgage and no idea who you are?

✿ You never know when something wonderful will happen to you—it could be today.

✿ You have billions of dust mites living in your pillow and feeding on your skin and earwax. Bet you want to get out of bed now!

✿ The more people you meet the more you will learn, so get out of bed and meet some interesting people. They may just change your life.

✿ Get out of the house and do something good for someone else.

✿ I have often found it is in the most unexpected of places or times that the biggest opportunities come so get out and look for something wonderful.

# CHALLENGE THE WAY YOU THINK

**Try an experiment with me. For every thought you have today and the rest of this week, I want you to actively challenge how you can say it as positively as possible. Monitor your internal dialogue and reprogram it.**

In spin class I kept thinking, 'Bugger this hurts'. I would quickly change it to, 'How powerful do I feel, shaping my legs the way I have, until now, only ever dreamed of?'

I changed 'I can't go on' to, 'I am now in a place that will transform my life. I am liberated. Push beyond and enjoy being a lean, mean, fat-burning machine'

When I did rowing and could barely breathe, instead of thinking 'I want to stop,' I thought, 'If I keep going, no matter how tired I am, I will be so much closer to my goals.'

How about you try these on for size:

In pump class: 'How incredible is it to actually feel the muscles growing?'

While boxing: 'I am such a powerful individual. I am pushing myself beyond my normal limitations.'

Running: 'Every step I take is one closer to the person I am becoming.'

When shopping: 'How great is it that I know the right foods to transform my body?'

Transformation begins within. Challenge every negative thought with a positive one and you will be amazed at how differently your day turns out.

Instead of getting home and saying 'I'm too tired to go and workout,' say, 'Isn't it great that I can give myself the incredible gift of a healthy life and a big rush of endorphins? I can't wait to overcome this feeling and be energised by what I am doing.'

'Isn't it amazing that this body I am wearing is no longer the true reflection of my life?'

'I am so powerful, making the right decisions.'

'This struggle is merely my body learning a better way. I am unbeatable.'

'I look forward to the pain after a workout, because it means my muscles are being repaired and are building a brand new body. Nothing worth having comes without effort.'

'I am grateful that people attempt to challenge me because it will make my victory so much sweeter. No matter how hard they try, they will NOT succeed in holding me back. I am learning just how strong I can be.'

'I am the living embodiment of who I want to be. Nothing will stop me from achieving my goals, not even this temporary setback.'

'This illness I am experiencing reminds me how precious health is, and when I get better I will savour every minute.'

'This feeling of loneliness reminds me to focus on my goals. The universe is keeping me free to become all that I can be, and when I am ready the right person will be there.'

'Today I choose to think happy positive thoughts. I am only focusing on the good, the best, the only outcome that will achieve my total happiness.'

'I am in control of my body, my mind, my heart, my mouth, my destiny and my spirit.'

From the mouth of Yoda: 'There is NO try. Only DO!'

# Like Sand Through an Hourglass

**For years, I got bogged down by the concept of how long it would take me to lose the weight I had put on. How could I possibly sustain what I needed to do to make that a reality?**

Sometimes I would start a new diet and be overwhelmed by the concept of continuing it day in and day out. One year seemed so far away, and what if it took me longer? I couldn't get my head around being healthy forever, so back to the pizzas and bottles of red wine I went.

The stupidest thing was that the time it would have taken me to get healthy came and went, and I was still fat and unhappy. 'Oh my God it's Christmas already?' I would think. 'I'm sure I would have lost 20 kilos by now but instead I have put on ten…now it will take me even longer.'

One day I decided to do things differently. I stopped worrying about time and I stopped worrying about being on a diet. I focused on good health: one day, one bite at a time. Some days were great; I had amazing control and determination. Others slipped by with a few beers and a battered sav, but they didn't roll into weeks of out-of-control eating.

This is now my life. This is your life too, and it's just a matter of time before your body reflects the changes you have made.

# What Good Will I Take From That?

**When life throws you a curve ball you can deal with it in two ways: fall face-first into whatever self-abusive coping mechanism you have taught yourself to use, or accept what is happening and nourish yourself with the lesson.**

Nourishment does not have to take the form of food; it can be delivered through a painful situation dealt with positively. You can do this with anything that has happened in your past, and turn your history into your future life story. That is when you truly grow.

Shift your focus from the painful events to the things you have learned from all that has happened to you. Nourish yourself with acceptance, understanding and empowerment and you will never feel the need to seek cuddles from cupcakes ever again.

Diamonds are formed under pressure. In the darkest of days, embrace the pain and make something precious with it.

# I Want That One!

**What is it that makes us—grown adults—want 'that one', right now?**

I recognise that baby voice. I hear when I go shopping and enter the lolly aisle, when I want takeaway, a night on the booze or a yummy cake in the bakery. Some part of our lives has become so selfish and badly programmed we think we can have whatever we want, whenever we want.

There was a time when the weekly shopping represented massive internal conflict—I just wanted to buy all the foods I had comforted myself with for the last five years, regardless of what they did to me. The 'now' of what they tasted like overcame the 'later' of what they felt like on my body.

I retrained my brain to accept that while I might not have it 'now', I could perhaps have it later. As I grew stronger I started tell myself 'I don't eat these foods.' I did not stop to look or consider the options.

That's not to say I never eat Tim Tams or Mint Slices, but I wait until they are somewhere I will only have one (for example, a morning tea at my kid's school—it's unlikely I will grab the whole packet, put my feet up on a desk and devour them all).

When you are about to make lunch, you might see the healthy low-fat soup you planned and find yourself 'wanting' something else. Catch that thought and make yourself stop fantasising about a world where you can indulge your whims on a daily basis.

Say to yourself: *I am not five years old. My world will continue if I don't have what I want right now. I am the grown up and I make decisions that are best for me.*

Acknowledge the child in you but learn to control that desire. Monitor who, out of the child and the adult, gets her way more often. If the balance needs to be redressed then give it a go. You may be pleasantly surprised at the results.

Nine years ago, I ate like a spoilt three-year old; I refused to eat vegetables. Today I sat down to homemade vegetable and lentil soup for the fourth day in a row and loved both the taste and what it does for my body. Ten years ago I decided to grow up and learn how to eat the right types of foods. You can too.

# Fat is Contagious

**I recently read an article claiming that if you spend time with fat people you will get fat, almost as if it were a contagious disease.**

The article created a furore. Fat people were incensed, saying they were discriminated against and misunderstood.

I, on the other hand, was challenged by the concept.

I have known what it is like to stand at a shop counter and be ignored. I have seen people look in my shopping basket and openly tut tut my choices, and I have had nasty words yelled at me from strangers in cars.

I have worked hard to transform my body and my life. I swapped negative thinking for empowered thoughts and actions. I have looked in a stranger's shopping basket filled with foods that keep them trapped in their self-abusive obesity and felt sorry for them. I didn't tut tut them, but I knew what they were doing to themselves and wanted to shake them until they understood they too could change for the better.

I have lived in both worlds. I would never ever go back to the way I was. Obesity was a filthy, destructive, scary, lonely, frightening, hateful place. I came to realise that to a degree, this article was right. Fat can be contagious. I'm not saying if you rub up against an overweight person on a bus you will wake up with a double chin. What I am saying is you become the kind of people you spend time with.

When I was obese, I spent a lot of my time with others who thought it okay to sit at home on a Saturday and binge. We would plan all the foods we would bring together and sit there like pigs in a sty. My fat friends kept me fat and made it OK to be that way.

If you want to learn something new you go to those who have the knowledge. When you want to become better, stronger, faster, and fitter, go to the people who are already that way. Learn from them, think like they do and copy them until you are just like them. Set your pace to someone else's stride, someone you aspire to be like. If you want to be fit and healthy then hang out with fit and healthy people.

Not every friendship I had during my obesity made it all the way through. Some people just would not accept the changes I made in my life. When it became obvious that some of those relationships were hurting me I had to let them go.

Language and behaviour are contagious. Energy is contagious. Knowledge cannot help but be shared. Be amongst those you want to be like most and transform in any way you can imagine. Set your pace to someone just ahead of you and try to keep up. Who knows, you may even overtake them one day. Wouldn't that be grand?

# THE ENEMY WITHIN

**Put your hand up if you have someone in your life who, every time you get on a roll, have a few good weeks or get really close to your goal, convinces you to crumble? They talk you into ditching training for a total junk food fest, downing cocktails named after naughty cowboys, following with a late night kebab fest.**

It's worse still when you realise that person is not your boyfriend, it's not your BFF, your mother-in-law or even the girls you share an office with. Your nightmare begins when you realise your worst enemy is you.

The good news is, knowing the enemy is the first step towards making sure they (meaning you) don't ruin all your hard work. It takes real commitment to win this but you can triumph. Ask anyone who has achieved their goals. It's so easy to talk yourself out of going for that run or worse, talking yourself into that second piece of cheesecake, but sticking to your guns can be done. Take heart.

I have found that carrying the burden of all you are doing can become challenging. You may need to give yourself a break, take responsibility away from yourself and ask for help. You need to be accountable for what you do, but maybe you can benefit from enlisting the help of a friend, training buddy or even a personal trainer. There is no shame in working with someone to achieve your goals.

You can do the same for them. If either of you have not heard from each other in two days then get on the phone, give a pep talk and remind yourselves of your goals. Be positive in all your language at all times, reminding each other how good you feel being focused and how good you will feel when you get to goal.  No-one wants an abusive coach; it does nothing to lift your spirit. Be nice to each other and kind to yourself.

You also enrol in charity events such as fun runs, bike days and walkathons. Once you commit your money, you are halfway across the finish line. Now all you have to do is turn up. Do it with a group and honour a friend who has struggled with whatever that charity represents. Do it with your children to be grateful for what they have. Raise money for a good cause, support someone you love and get fit all at the same time.

# It's Sarong Size

**When I was size-challenged (okay, you can use the word 'ginormous'), I still had special events to attend. These were always horrifying times for me, as I could never find anything to wear.**

In the end I stopped going out and made my excuses when these events came up. I hid away from the world and drowned my feelings in even more food. I even talked my half sister out of having me as a bridesmaid because I didn't think a dress would fit me. Talk about regret!

When I just could not get out of something, I started wearing a sari—one big long piece of material wrapped up around me like a big fat mummy. I might as well have rolled myself up in a floor rug—at least if I had a few drinks it would make lying on the floor a whole lot easier.

Off I went to these events, dressed like an Indian woman. I was trying to be all 'New-Age' and 'goddess-like', but I was uncomfortable, wrapped up in ill-fitting clothes and wishing, just wishing things were different. But I would still drink 27 beers and eat everything on the table, only stopping short of consuming the presents and the guests.

The reality is I will always be a reflection of the way I treat my body. When I eat crap my body will respond, if I don't exercise I turn to jelly and it is only ME who is to blame for that. If you are fat and have a doughnut in your hand then it's not cause you are big-boned, it's because you've got a bloody doughnut in your hand.

Have a look at your life as it is right now. What is stopping you from achieving your goals? It could be a really simple list:

- ❀ Drink too much
- ❀ Eat junk food three times a week
- ❀ Skip breakfast
- ❀ Snack too often
- ❀ Eat creamy pastas all the time
- ❀ Work too much and don't make time to exercise
- ❀ Don't make time for anything good for me

- ✿ Wrong priorities
- ✿ Lazy
- ✿ Not ready—BS alert!
- ✿ Allow boyfriend to distract me (double BS!)
- ✿ Etc.

If you spend a few minutes attaching how you are with what you do (or don't do), you can find solutions. It's not rocket science—you can work out what to do in five minutes or less.

For example:

- ✿ Drink too much? Drink water instead.
- ✿ Eat rubbish? Find healthier versions.
- ✿ Skip breakfast? Eat brekkie (der!).
- ✿ Snack too often? Snack less.
- ✿ Eat creamy pastas? Eat less or make healthier versions.
- ✿ Work too much and don't make time? Make time.
- ✿ Don't make time? Make time.
- ✿ Wrong priorities? Change them.
- ✿ Lazy? Get motivated.
- ✿ Not ready? Yes you are.
- ✿ Allow boyfriend to distract me? Dump him. OK, maybe not, but stop blaming others and take responsibility.

You can apply this technique to anything you want to change in your life. When you start to break it down it becomes less overwhelming, more manageable and not as fuelled by emotion. Take responsibility—you are what you eat and you are what you don't eat. Your body reflects the way you treat yourself. So treat yourself well and enjoy the rest of your healthy, well-dressed life.

# DON'T GIVE UP

**Tanzanian marathon runner John Stephen Ahkwari had the incredible honour of representing his country in the 1968 Olympics in Mexico City. At some point in the 42km run, Ahkwari stumbled to the ground and seriously injured his leg and knee. When most would give up, he instead allowed his leg to be bandaged and continued the race, running and walking, running and walking for another two hours after the fall.**

Nearly two hours after his fall, Ahkwari stopped for a second outside a floodlit stadium, channelling the last of his reserves to get him across the finish line. The stadium was almost empty, and the spectators who were there came for an entirely different event—the marathon had long since finished. However, they stood and cheered as history was made—not for the fastest runner but certainly the most courageous.

Ahkwari was now buoyed by the support in the stadium, the cheers giving him strength to take his agonised walk and turn it into a tentative but determined run, this time literally dragging his injured leg behind him but refusing to stop until he crossed the finish line.

The most important part of this story is in Ahkwari's answer to the one question asked by many: 'Why did you keep running?'

His response, in its beautiful simplicity, was this: 'My country did not send me 5000 miles to start the race, they sent me 5000 miles to finish the race.'

Don't give up when you mess up! Imagine if all the athletes who did not win medals just gave up without ever coming back to compete again. They train for years and years for that one moment, and all it takes is one slip, trip or fall for it to slip from their grasp.

What do we see them do time and time again? They simply get up and go on.

They don't sit there in a heap of recriminations and anger, making a nest for themselves to wallow in the awfulness of the 'failure'. They get up and finish what they need to and focus on the next competition.

The only way you can fail at transforming your life is if you give up. As long as you pick yourself up after a fall and get back into the race, you have an excellent opportunity to succeed. The only way you can fail is if you quit—and quitting is not an option!

# Don't Eat Your Way to Even More Unhappiness

**Why is it that when a guy is first interested in us we have no problem taking ourselves to the gym twice a day? We spend hours making sure we look hot and don't we just know it! Confidence oozes out of our fresh, acne-free pores. And then the second he doesn't call, we find ourselves in a bucket of triple chocolate rocky road ice cream followed by a box of Cadbury Favourites—and that's just a snack.**

How many times have you not gotten that job and eaten a pizza? Not got a text from that cutie you party-pashed the other night and eaten a packet of Tim Tams? Argued with a friend and fallen into Hungry Jacks?

As I got better at coping without bingeing, I did not succumb to this kind of eating. I thought about that double beef and bacon burger and then pictured it on my thighs the next time I met a guy. I took myself to the gym and did a killer workout where I told the trainer to push me until I wanted to vomit. I walked out so much taller and prouder of myself.

Then there was the argument with my friend that had me almost unconsciously walking the aisles of the supermarket until I stood staring at the chockies and drooling. Instead of buying them, I took myself to The Body Shop, got a yummy loofah, decadent bath milk and a face mask, ran a bath, lit a candle, played some music and treated myself to some good old-fashioned pampering. Came out feeling and smelling like a goddess and reminded myself that I deserve the very best of everything, including friends.

Close the fridge door, get yourself to the gym, run yourself a bath—just do something nice for yourself and see how much better that feels than stuffing your face. Realise that you are a goddess, and goddesses do not binge eat, they flex their muscles, wield their swords and chase the demons away.

# So You've Lost Your Mojo?

**Ever had one of those weeks where you just want to crawl into a hole and disappear? When you feel like the light at the end of the tunnel has been snuffed out?**

Everyone has bad times, and we've all done things we regret or wish we'd done differently. But you cannot change what has already happened, all you can do is learn from it.

Do you remember a time when you felt free and full of promise, in control, on top of the world, young, strong, capable of achieving your dreams and like no-one was going to stand in your way? During the bad times it can feel like you have lost your mojo.

Remember, three steps forward and one step back is still two steps forward. When this time becomes the past you will look back and laugh it off. You can only appreciate the good times by living through the bad!

You have a choice: spend your days depressed and wishing things were different, or put your energy into changing your life.

Accept where you are, take a deep breath and, slowly but surely, put one foot in front of the other. Walk away from this time and never come back. You can do this!

The only person who can save you is you! The only person who can change your life is you! Be bold. Think big, because if you persevere, no matter how hard things get, you will achieve everything your heart desires.

Now spread your wings and fly!

# BELIEVE

**As host of *The Biggest Loser* I had an opportunity to fly to a remote little mining town called Dysart. It is basically built around a big hole in the ground. It took one big plane, two small ones and a three-hour car ride to get there. Even the tumbleweed is lonely in this place.**

I was there as the guest of honour at a Health and Wellness festival put on by the mining company. Part of the program was a performance by some of the local kids who had formed a dance troupe. I sat at the front and watched a biggish girl dancing in the front line, giving it all she had. When I say 'biggish' I don't really mean 'big', but for a dancer she definitely stood out from the rest of the group. Despite her big smile, I knew she would be subjected to a degree of teasing. Kids can be so cruel for even the slightest difference.

But what I noticed more was that despite her size, she was by far the best dancer in the group—and not only that, she was having the time of her life. My gaze was irresistibly drawn to her because the joy in her eyes was compelling and thoroughly mesmerising. She reminded me so much of myself when I was her age.

I grew up in small town called Mummulgum (not Bubblegum!), Northern New South Wales, home of Beef Week and the yearly honouring and crowning of the Beef Queen. The closest 'city' was Casino, which was not really a city and had no casino.

I was lucky enough, despite the isolation, to be able to do ballet and jazz. Even though I was not as big as the girl on the Dysart stage, and not big by any other than anorexic ballet standards, I was continually overlooked by my ballet teacher, ignored by the skinny ballet-stars-to-be and told repeatedly I was too fat to be successful in any field of entertainment.

My parents gave my brother and me 10 dollars a week pocket money. My brother bought the latest records and I bought extra ballet lessons on top of the two my parents already paid for.

My brother and I each had a cow and every year they gave birth to calves, which we could sell and use the money however we wanted. My brother bought records. I paid the fees to become part of the eisteddfod group and financed the cost of all of my costumes.

I was, sadly, denied the opportunity to compete in the solo eisteddfod category. My teacher told me she was not going to waste her time on someone who would never go anywhere. For the Christmas shows I was never picked for solos, duets, quintets or even the corps de ballet. I was always put way up the back, I always had the smallest part possible (tree), my body was always pinched and prodded as I squeezed into a tutu two sizes too small.

I didn't care; I loved dance. It was the closest thing I could get to being in the limelight, performing and leaving the small country world behind. I spent hours a day dancing around the house, composing whole ballets in my mind, and collected little porcelain ballerinas. I dreamed of a life outside of my tiny backwater town where so many horrible things had happened to me. It was my escape.

We did exams every year, judged by an independent authority overseen by the British Ballet Organisation. Fail, Pass, Commended, Highly Commended and Honours were the grades given. Usually only one or two girls in each class got Honours.

I'll never forget the last exam I ever did. We had to perform our final set dance routine in pairs in front of the examiners. The partners were determined alphabetically which meant I was destined to dance next to Natalie Sharp: the best dancer in the school. Natalie spent her holidays training with the Australian Ballet. I spent weeks crying with the thought of looking like a 100-kilo gallumphing elephant next to her. I was doomed.

The day of the exam, a calm came over me and I decided it didn't matter who I danced next to. I decided to do exactly what I had done every other time: throw away my fear, fall into the music and just be me.

And I did just that. I didn't care that she was beside me, in fact I'm not sure I noticed her. I moved to the beat of my own heart, my soul took flight and I went wherever it was I went each and every time I danced. I was free to be me.

A few weeks later the exam results came in the mail and we nervously awaited our fate. I knew it would be my last exam as I was moving to Sydney to go to drama school in the hope of making it big. I hoped for Highly Commended. My teacher said I would be lucky to get that and to prepare myself.

She read out my name and hesitated on the result. My heart fell to the pit of my stomach.

She squinted as if she could not read what was written, and looked up at me in surprise. I knew then that I had failed.

'Honours?' she read, more of a question than a statement.

'Sorry?' I asked, not quite believing what she had said.

'Honours,' she repeated, shaking her head and holding out my certificate. And as I walked up to receive my medal she continued. 'Honestly, I don't know what you do in those examination rooms that you don't do in front of me.'

I took my certificate and said, 'Miss, what I do in the exam room is what I do every week here in this class. You just can't see it cause you can't see ME. You can't see beyond what you believe I am—too fat, too heavy and not talented—but when I dance away from you I can be as good as I can be. I believe in myself and other people can see that. I know I will never be a ballerina but for now dancing is all I have, and when I hear that music my heart sings and maybe that is what makes me good and maybe that is what the examiners like: they see someone who loves what they do and who doesn't care what others think. And most importantly of all, when they look at me they have not already made up their minds about me.'

OK, I didn't really say that, but when I rewrite my history I always say that and so much more.

I moved to Sydney, studied drama and dance and to this day still take classes. The entire experience made me stronger and certainly prepared me for the brutality of the entertainment industry. You have not seen the best of me yet (I am like a good wine and improve with age), but what you see is an open heart and a desire to dance through life.

Never judge yourself or someone else by how they look. Never make up your mind about anyone's ability or limitations, including your own. Never give up and always dance, laugh, sing and run no matter how good or bad anyone thinks you are—including yourself.

Oh and by the way, I pulled aside the biggish girl in the dance troupe and told her I thought she rocked more than anything or anyone else.

# 101 THINGS THAT MAKE ME ME AND MAKE YOU YOU!

**This is a beautiful exercise created by one of my girls on Healthy Body Club. She'd done a lot of soul searching, then one day decided to chronicle 101 things that made her who she is today. It was amazing to peek into someone's life so intimately, and we all quickly found we couldn't resist the urge to do the same.**

You get a real sense of where you have come from, what you have conquered and what you believe in. Putting the past in the past and moving forward is empowering.

Here is an example of my list and how I used it to empower my current life. You can do the same.

1.  I was adopted. I am grateful for it making me the person I am today.

2.  I stayed in the hospital for six weeks because of ear infections. My adopted mother didn't visit me because she said that she couldn't bear to see me then leave me. What the? I can't help but think that these days they would not release a baby to someone so selfish. This makes me a better mother to my own son.

3.  I spent the first seven years of my life in suburban Sydney.

4.  I was a very active kid. I did ballet, callisthenics, swimming and tennis. This reminds me I was not always overweight. I have the power to evolve.

5.  I was a champion swimmer. Had we not moved to the country I might have swum in the Olympics. I now want to win a medal in shooting. A medal may be my destiny but like life, sometimes the path you tread is different to the one you imagined.

6.  My favourite time of the year was Firecracker day. We used to build a huge bonfire in the park at the end of the street. I'll never forget the year we burnt my 'dad'. He had given his clothes to make the dummy for the top of the fire. It was truly weird cause I didn't really like my dad too much. Rituals mean more to us than we think.

7.  My dad was a workaholic. He always brought home fish and chips on a Friday night. This shaped my emotional attachment to hot chips.

8.  I never really saw him much until we moved to the country when I was eight.

9.  Then he became an abusive alcoholic. He used to say he wished he'd never adopted me. Sometimes the feeling is mutual.

10. I hated moving to the country because there was nothing to do. At first.

11. I loved ballet and eventually convinced my parents to let me take it up again in the local town. I came alive when the music started.

12. I loved my first pair of pointe shoes. They were so precious to me and best of all they were soft baby pink!

13. I was never skinny, but definitely not fat. My ballet teacher always told my mother I had to lose weight.

14. I always got Honours in my ballet exams.

15. My brother was a champion sports star. He was brilliant at soccer and cricket and played rep at both. He was going to be a champion. Life is what we make of it.

16. We both got 10 dollars a week pocket money. He got to spend his, I had to pay for my own ballet lessons. I never understood why but I learned that if you want something enough, you can make it happen.

17. He used to buy records. I had no money to spend so I borrowed books from the library instead. You don't always need money to survive.

18. I am a speed reader. I devoured books. I hated that you could only borrow three books at a time because we only ever went into town once a week. I could read 10 books a week. I was always hungry for more.

19. That's why I started to write. It was just as good as reading if not better. It also filled up a lot of time. Being 'bored' in the country was a creative gift.

20. I loved roller skating. I had white boots with red wheels. They were unreal. I used to skate up and down my rumpus room to my dad's rock 'n' roll records. I had to skate smoothly or the records would jump. Then Olivia Newton John did Xanadu

and that was the only song I skated to. When Olivia asked me to walk the Great Wall of China with her and her friends there was no way I could refuse despite being a single mum and having no idea how I would do it. That was what Oprah calls an 'A-ha moment'.

21.  I loved and still love horses. I had nine of them.

22.  My dad hated horses. Horses hated my dad. Animals are very smart.

23.  I was the only person who could ride my horse. She was mental. Just like me. It's nice to know you are not alone.

24.  I used to pretend I was a teenage detective. I loved Nancy Drew and Trixie Belden books. I wished I was Honey Wheeler, the rich kid who lived next door. One day I will write a mystery book that will be a best seller.

25.  My brother was the star of our family. Everyone loved him.

26.  My nana used to say that because he was so good looking he would have whatever he wanted in life. I learnt that no-one knows the future and you have the power to create your own.

27.  She used to tell me that because I was plain I would have to work really hard to get anything I wanted. I hated it at the time but realise now it was a blessing, because no matter how hard things get I never ever give up because I always knew and believed I would have to work hard.

28.  I remember being as young as eight saying I wanted to be an author and an actress. I did exactly what I said I would do. It's time to set some new goals.

29.  I also remember people telling me that was a silly dream because hardly anyone made it.

30.  I vividly remember my reply: 'Well someone has to make it so why not me?'

31.  I had my first poem published in the Herald when I was 10. I made six dollars. It was awesome. I had my next one published one month later and made five. That was when I started to write every day of every week. I have never stopped in one form or another. I didn't do it for the money, I did it so that someone in my life acknowledged my existence to be worth something.

32. My school teacher abused me from the age of eight to 10. Three years. It was hell.

33. He used to pick on me in class and make me cry in front of everyone.

34. I used to get into trouble for things I had not done so he could send me to the office to 'punish me'. He punished me in the most disgusting way. I gave evidence against him years later but they could not prosecute due to the lack of solid evidence. Pity there were no hidden cameras in my underpants. It has made me vigilant in the protection of my own son.

35. The best thing about the farm was the river. When it flooded, the waterhole filled up and we swam in it every day.

36. My best friend lived next door. Next door was a 15-minute horse ride away. Her dad was killed by the horn of a cow. It made me realise that even though my dad was an abusive alcoholic at least I had one.

37. My other best friend was killed in the Blue Mountains train wreck. So was her son. It was devastating. Life is short and precious. We often forget that.

38. My best friend when I was 25 had epilepsy and she suffocated on her pillow one night. My heart broke the night she died. It really hurt. Sometimes I live life for the one she lost.

39. My adopted mother was a tyrant. She made me the best mother on the planet.

40. She used to beat me with hair brushes, belts, canes…whatever she could get her hands on. I do not and will not beat my child.

41. She had Obsessive Compulsive Disorder. Everything had to be lined up and in all sorts of orders. I live like a pig. I now need to realise I don't need to be the opposite to all that she was. I'm still learning, healing and growing every day.

42. She used to go through my room and leave nasty notes in my drawers.

43. She used to count the biscuits in the tin (any wonder I later binged on them).

44. She used to cry all the time. Now I think she didn't mean to be so horrible, she was probably clinically depressed.

45. She used to eat bags of lollies but never share them.

46. Sometimes she would say to me 'Don't call me mother. I'm not your mother.'

47. She also used to say that if I tried to find my birth mother she would put her head in the oven and kill herself, and that I would have to live with that.

48. One day I did it anyway (found my birth mother). My adopted mother did not come go through with her threat, and I found a long-last part of myself.

49. Freaky thing was, I had worked in my birth mother's theatre restaurant the year before and already knew her.

50. One year later my birth mother passed away. Kind of sadly ironic that she was the one who took her life and not the one who had threatened to for years. The official verdict is suicide but I have and will never accept that. I miss her every day. No matter how bad things get, I will never kill myself. That is the gift she left me: the strength to go on.

51. In high school I had a crush on my best friend's brother. His name was Mathew Pollard and I adored him. He was my first love. I never told him and he never kissed me. He was my date for my debut. In my mind I married him that night.

52. The first guy I ever tongue pashed was Greg Isaac. He had beautiful green eyes and I adored him so much I wrote a book about him when I was fifteen. He tasted like Vegemite and bit my lip the first time we kissed. I broke it off because I was scared he'd want to kiss me again.

53. I loved high school.

54. I was smart and in all the top classes.

55. I loved English and hated maths. My poor son has suffered the same fate.

56. I was the number one kid in English every year until Brett McCleod from America came to our school. He beat me by one mark, once. He never beat me again. I hated him. He was my nemesis. I also flourished because I worked harder than I had ever worked before. He was my Professor Moriarty.

57. I was blessed by two teachers who transformed my life. They made me believe in myself. I adored them. Thomas Gray and Gary Whale: I owe you.

58. One of them talked me out of a locked toilet when I was booed off stage during a performance. That taught me the fundamentals of the entertainment industry.

59. That same person told me I had the talent to make it. I believed him, I went for it and I did make it. This one's for you Thomas x.

60. I kept in touch with both of them.

61. Thomas died of leukaemia. He had not done all he should have. Life is cruel and short. Act now.

62. I used to be a clown for kids' parties. I loved it and was really good.

63. I write poetry. I love to perform it.

64. I write really good song parodies.

65. One day I want to write best-selling crime thriller novels like James Patterson.

66. My adoptive mother has not spoken to me since I gave evidence to the police about my school teacher molesting me. I will always be there for my son no matter what.

67. I lost my virginity to my cousin's best friend. He lasted 30 seconds and I felt ripped off.

68. I loved my cousin for years. He was not really my cousin (no blood relation) and we kissed every time we got together from the age of eight. We continued a relationship right up until I was 19.

69. I was in the movie where Russell Crowe met Danielle Spencer. Russ was mean and nasty for no good reason. I never understand why people are like that. He is not the only person I have worked with who is like that.

70. I had bulimia and anorexia for years. I am a survivor.

71. I got down to about 43 kilos. I used to say to women that I wanted to be as thin as them, not realising I was thinner. They used to say, 'you're sick.' They were right.

72. I ran a triathlon for the very first time. I came last. It was fantastic. I have my sights set on a marathon.

73. My first dog was called Mandy. The first street I lived in was Bruce. That makes

my porn name Mandy Bruce. If I ever leave things on forums I write under that name. I write anonymously under that name too. Guess it's not so anonymous now!

74.  I love comedy. I gave up doing stand-up when my birth mum died. I gave everything but life up. I became a drug-taking, alcoholic, binge-eating recluse. It resulted in my obesity. The upside: a whole new career path. What I learnt: not everything that feels bad is.

75.  One of my few unrealised goals is to do a comedy show on TV. My life is not over.

76.  I also want to be in a musical like *Cats* or *Chicago*.

77.  I love to sing and occasionally write jazz. I have an album of jazz and spoken word called *Sexual Encounters*. It's hard to find.

78.  Even though Kai was not planned he is the best thing that has ever happened to me.

79.  He has Asperger's syndrome. Sometimes it is so hard you don't know how you are going to go on. Other days it is pure joy. It is what it is and I will always try to make the most of what we have been given.

80.  I love to paint. I paint a lot these days. I give the paintings to charities to auction off. I'm not very confident but getting better and next year I am going to have a show. Scary.

81.  I love anything pink.

82.  I love Healthy Body Club. Even though it doesn't make money it helps a lot of people.

83.  I love hot chips.

84.  I hate that I love hot chips.

85.  I will never ever be obese again. Except when I'm 80 and can eat whatever I want and never exercise.

86.  Actually I want to be one of those grannies doing triathlons.

87. I have no family but wish I did. (Since writing that I started building a relationship with my birth mother's family. I have an aunt, a grandma and two cousins I absolutely adore and more I am yet to get to know.)

88. I have a photo of a man I believe to be my birth father but don't know how to find him to do a DNA test. There is always so much more to do in life.

89. I believe that when things are the very worst they could be there is something wonderful on the other side of it. You just have to ride it out to discover what it may be. Sometimes you have to make it wonderful yourself other times it just is.

90. One day I want to live in France.

91. One day I will be on *Oprah*.

92. I want to be the next Oprah. I have never had problems dreaming big.

93. I drink too much.

94. I love a good laugh.

95. I love Austin Powers. Kai calls him Oscan Powers.

96. If I hadn't have gone into drama and writing I would have worked with disabled children. I adore them.

97. My favourite book of all time is 'Tis.

98. I don't regret getting fat, I just regret the length of time I stayed fat.

99. You wouldn't believe it but I am a loner. My shrink says it's because I have lost too many people I love.

100. My life has just begun.

101. I truly believe that the only ingredient needed to succeed is to never give up. No matter what happens.

I cannot tell you how free doing this makes you. You can step aside from yourself and see how even the smallest of events have shaped you.

Feel free to revisit your list again and again, reminding yourself that you are not a victim of the past and you don't need to live in the shadow of what has happened to you. You are free to let go, free to grow into the beautiful human being that you are and live the life you deserve.

# 'I Feel Fat'

**'I'm just so fat!' How many times have you heard someone utter those words when they don't need to lose weight at all?**

Having struggled to lose over 50 kilos from my 160 centimetre frame, I find myself incensed when I hear someone say they are fat when it's plainly obvious they are not. But I too thought I was fatter than I was at various times in my life. I too have obsessed about my weight until everyone around me was sick to death of hearing, 'Do I look fat in this dress? Does my bum look big in this? Do these shoes make me look like I have cankles?'

I would hereby like to apologise to all the friends and family I have bored over the years with my constant groaning at my body. I am sorry.

When I worked in radio, one of our 'chicks' in the 'rock mobiles' got a job on *Home and Away*. She was absolutely gorgeous and stick thin (those two things are not related), probably a size 8 at the most. She was with us for three more months before she went off to become a big star, and during that time we saw her whittle her frame down to a tiny size six. We would be chowing down on bacon and egg McMuffins and she would be snacking on carrot sticks for breakfast.

I was flabbergasted. I couldn't understand why someone so beautiful could think they needed to lose weight. She said it was because all the other girls were so thin and that TV made you look seven kilos heavier (it does) and she didn't want to be the fattest actress on the show. She reasoned that she would feel better about herself if she did it. She was stunningly beautiful, had a fantastically gorgeous and successful boyfriend, a loving family, an extremely successful career—but she was not happy and blamed it on her weight. Go figure!

The saddest part of that story is that the woman in question, having hated her body for so many years, died a premature death ravaged with cancer. Life is so cruel. She was beautiful and talented and very much loved by anyone who ever came into contact with her. She struggled with her body, self-esteem and the pressure to always get thinner, and for what?

I read an article last year, released on International No Diet Day, which said 60 per cent of women in the healthy weight range felt they would be happier if they lost five kilos. It would be good to fit into that sexy pair of jeans we have coveted for so long, but to hold off on being happy until you do is a waste of your precious life.

I have come to learn that losing weight will not actually make me any happier. Having been anorexic and weighing in at 40 kilos, I not only thought I was still fat but believed that if I lost more weight, only then would I find happiness.

But let's not be too harsh too quickly, because there is a very real psychological illness called Body Dysmorphia Disorder. The sufferer has a preoccupation with a perceived defect in their appearance. It can manifest in many forms: severe dislike for the nose, face, breasts, etc. People suffering from this disorder are so convinced of their need to change that they justify people's comments to fit with their obviously distorted view of themselves. For example, if someone were to say that they look great, the sufferer would reason that they were just saying it to make them feel better.

The reality is the number of sufferers of BDD is quite low. Dr J Kevin Thomson (author of *Body Image Disturbance: Assessment and Treatment*, Pergamon Press, 1990), says the disorder is rare, affecting only one to two per cent of the general population and affecting men and women equally.

So where does this leave us obsessing about the size of our thighs? What is healthy? What is obsession? How can we know if we really need to lose some weight, or if it's about something else entirely? And either way, dysmorphic or just plain unhappy about your size, how do you go about changing the way you see and feel about yourself?

I have had a range of eating disorders. I was anorexic, then bulimic and then I just plain binged until well, there just wasn't enough food left to feed me. When I finally approached weight loss the healthy way, I observed (and worked on) all my past behaviours.

After losing about 35 kilos, I wandered into my shrink's office utterly defeated. I told her how fat I felt and that no amount of weight loss was going to make me feel any different, because at 40 kilos I had still felt the same way.

My shrink asked me to draw my body. I did and it repulsed me. She then drew her version of me and it was about half the size. She told me that was my real size and the way I drew it was the way I saw myself. She always says to me, 'just because you feel a certain way does not mean you are a certain way.' I saw myself as fat no matter what size I was.

Through therapy I discovered that my 'feeling fat' was all centred on how I felt about myself. When asked what fat meant to me I came up with a list including feeling unloved, not being good enough, not being successful, being unhappy. I believed that if I were 'thin' (whatever that was), I would be happy, successful and loved.

Now, with a much healthier way of viewing life, I realise how ridiculous that was. My lack of self-esteem had attached itself to my negative body image and my 'weight' subsequently became the agenda for all my woes in life. It distracted me from the real issues I needed to deal with.

I went on to concentrate on what would make me happy, loved, and successful. I diverted my negative thoughts and energy into actively fulfilling myself on every level.

I was so busy being happy that I didn't have the time, energy or inclination to dwell on what I didn't like about my body, and subsequently learnt to like myself the way I was. Ironically I lost another 25 kilos without even trying, but that didn't actually make me any happier or more successful. I found the fat days disappearing into my past well before I was no longer 'fat'.

These days I recognise the occasional fat day for what it is. The first thing I do is a reality check. I remind myself that I am not as fat as I was or as fat as I think I am. Then I ask myself what I am really feeling. Usually it relates to something that is not going well in my life. I go into action mode and focus all my energy on making whatever is wrong, right.

What this means to you:

1. You are not as fat as you think you are.

2. If you think being 'thin' or even 'thinner' will make you happy then you are headed for disaster. Getting happy is the only thing that will make you happy.

3. If you want to change your body, change the way you think about yourself. Love yourself and the body will follow.

4. Before you decide to lose weight, know whether you're in the healthy weight range. Go to www.mydr.com.au and measure your BMI. This is your Body Mass Index and it gives you a healthy weight range for your height.

5. Be nice to yourself. If you want to change the shape of your body, join a gym, eat healthily and treat yourself well. Your body will change over time. It's not a race. The slower you do it the longer it will stay off.

6. When you look in the mirror, concentrate on the things you like. Spend no time thinking about what you want to change. The reality is that no matter what you change on the outside you are still the same within. Be happy with that.

7. Dr Nutcase used to say to me, 'If you don't like your reflection then don't look at it. Only look when you are ready to see and say good things.' It not only changed the way I saw myself but it also changed the way I live.

8. If you find yourself obsessing about your body, ask someone you trust to assess whether you are being realistic. If you are in doubt seek professional help.

9. If your happiness is totally centred on your body, seek counselling and work on learning to love yourself.

10. Love yourself. Every day.

You are so much more than your body shape. You are a beautiful, spirited human being filled with life and with so much to give. Our bodies constantly change from the day we are born to the day we die. Focus on your inner beauty. Look in the mirror and love who you are. Decide for the next week that every time you see yourself you will think and say something good. I guarantee you by the week's end a peace will start to enter your life.

# Light at the End of the Tunnel

**There have been many times when I have stared into the dark chasm of despair. I have held a razor in one hand and pills in the other and wondered which I would use first.**

I have sat on the edge of cliffs and wished the wind would take me away and prayed that I might have the 'courage' to push myself off.

I have cried all night, all day, all week, all month, eaten enough for five people, smoked for five and drunk for ten and yet I have still found room for despair and loneliness. Excess did nothing for me.

There have been times when I have thought 'Why me?' then beaten myself up for being so selfish. Thinking badly of myself did nothing for me.

I have loved food, hated food, eaten food, avoided food, thought about food, not thought about food and none of it made my life any more complete.

I have lost friends, buried my mother, had dreams destroyed, been homeless, loveless and penniless. I have hurt others, been hurt and witnessed my son's heart broken at too young an age. I have come from nothing, had nothing, been nothing and felt nothing.

None of this has killed me.

In 12 months I lost all that I owned, had my integrity questioned, career stalled, been broken and battered and abused by both strangers and those I held dear to me.

None of this killed me.

Through the generosity of friends and strangers, I managed to keep myself and my son off the street by 'living' in 23 'homes' in nine months. Some might think that unbearable, we called it an adventure.

I have saved my life, changed my life, and healed my life. This is what I call living.

I sit here today thankful for all that has happened to me—good and bad. Every single moment of my life, both in darkness and light, has been precious to me. I know that whenever it is darkest or hardest, whenever I am hurting the most, I am learning the most and it cannot kill me.

To let go and embrace 'the journey' is one of the most powerful insights you can ever have.

The calm you feel when you know the upswing is just moments away is liberating. If you know anything about Newton's theory (that everything has an equal and opposite reaction) then you can put the chocolate cake down and know everything is going to be okay. The peace you feel knowing the light is just a few more steps ahead is empowering.

Your only choice when things get tough is to just keep going. Stopping to look back, or punish yourself for being human (because we all have these moments in our lives) or to lend a hand in sabotaging your goals will do nothing for you.

There is no true and lasting happiness to be found in a bottle, no peace in self-hatred and certainly no life-fulfilling moments at the bottom of a bucket of KFC.

True happiness lies in taking the next step and knowing it is taking you someplace better.

# THE FINAL WORD

**Have you taken the first step? Have you eaten a healthy meal, drunk some water, phoned a friend? Did you get in touch with your feelings and find it didn't kill you? Discovered you can do more than you ever thought you could? Learnt something new? Had a bad day and came back fighting, happy in the knowledge you were better, fitter, faster, smarter or all of the above?**

And how did it feel? Easier than you first thought? It really doesn't have to be as hard or impossible to achieve as the dieting industry makes out. You can do anything you set your mind to.

Are you thinner? Maybe, maybe not (yet), but I bet you are healthier and happier, and you may even love and believe in yourself a little bit more. You have everything you need to succeed inside of you.

Sort out your head and your heart and your body will follow. Work hard but don't be hard on yourself. Be good but don't expect yourself to be perfect. Think big but do it one small bite at a time.

*Don't get what you are given—take what you want!*

*This is YOUR life so LIVE IT FULLY. Start now. The rest of your new healthier, happier existence is waiting for you.*

*THIS IS THE BEGINNING.*

# Acknowledgements

When I get to this part in the book I always feel like I am at the Oscars and I've just been awarded Best Actress (perhaps Drama Queen would be more appropriate!). I've tripped up the stairs, torn my frock, I'm crying and babbling and I have completely forgotten my speech, thanked my weirdo neighbour, long-lost dead aunt and my seven cats, thanked none of the people I should have and have tried to recite a badly written poem by Russel Crowe whilst the band are playing me off.

Oh, the pressure. Okay, here goes.

In NO particular order I would like to thank: my darling Kaizziepops, my new/old family including my 'sistahs' Simmy Button, Corina Rocky Rochester, Nan and Barb for welcoming me in, Aunty and Uncle Muff Jaq and Jase, Inspector Muff for being a true Muff to the end, J Muff for ferrying Kai and I to the queen and back and Queen Muff.

Leeza Gibbons who made me believe I could do it and supported me in ways above and beyond.

Mardi 'got tickkat' Croke for always picking up the pieces; Loz and Bon for being my USA buds; Bryan Wiseman who literally kept Kai and I off the streets during the tough times; The Real McQuades—Emily, Jackson, Jon, Steve, Pete AND Tracy—for loving my little boy so much; Sarah Savic and Lauren Moran for being inspirational, motivational, caring, genuine generous and undying in their support of me and Healthy Body Club.

Vivicca, my crazy and incredibly hilarious US friend and sistah; Uncle Ian who always survives the closet cleanup; none other than my manager, the infamous Max Markson for keeping me on the straight and narrow (well that's stretching it); Martin The Sarge Gleave for always being there for Kai and me, and Bootsie (see I did thank my dog).

Yvette and Andy Gent for their endless support and tireless effort in keeping Healthy Body Club alive; Lou Lou Pollard—another of my sistahs; Nyrie Dodd, Jules Jones; Demi, my sistah from anotha motha; Matt 'Heffy' Dillon, Cowboy Husby Adam Sutton, Breezy, Bublez.

Dr Nutcase, who really helped me heal my life and whose voice lives inside my head to this day (another issue altogether!).

I also would like to say a huge eternal thank you to Dr Norris at Silkwood Medical in Bondi Junction Sydney for my absolute life-changing surgery. Carrying that extra flesh around really was a burden, both physically and emotionally and your gentleness, passion, support, kindness, generosity and of course expertise have transformed my life and body. (www.silkwoodmedical.com.au)

Nestlé—and Faith Yi in particular for being such a great support (www.meals.com). Stephen Steneker from www.grox.com.au who rebuilt and kept Healthy Body Club going all these years.

I want to thank Fremantle, Channel Ten and *Biggest Loser* for giving me a huge boost towards fulfilling my dreams. A huge thank you to everyone who helped Kai and me with our US Visas allowing us to fully stalk, sorry I mean chase, Oprah: Michelle and Michael from 11:11 who took in a complete stranger, Stuart Krasnow, Lawrence Yarwood, John Gregory, Carl Fennessey, Cathie Scott, David Mott, Melissa Gear, Eva Orner, Eric Feig, Harlan Freedman, Dave Broome, David Lyle, Mike Goldman, Rob Logan, and everyone else who helped get us here and supported us on the journey.

And my mum, Kaylene Rochester, for giving me life. Love you Mum, hope I make you proud.

Oh and if per chance I haven't thanked you here, it's because you were so important to me I am saving my thank you for the dedication in my next book, name in the front of course. Gulp. Thank you and bless you all!

# HEALTHY BODY CLUB

Healthy
BodyClub.com.au

Tired of struggling and doing it on your own?

Join Ajay Rochester's Healthy Body Club for FREE and get 3 months of support, guidance, friendship, motivation and inspiration.

Go to www.healthybodyclub.com.au and type in promo code:  5MINNH to claim your free membership.

You are not alone!

3 1170 00867 5302